# THE CONSONANT PHONEMES OF PROTO-EAST-CUSHITIC (PEC):
## A FIRST APPROXIMATION

by

Hans-Jürgen Sasse
University of Munich

This paper is a preliminary attempt to reconstruct the consonant system of Proto-East-Cushitic (PEC), one of the four branches of the Cushitic family. Data are taken from some twenty-odd languages including unpublished material on a variety of hitherto little known languages. After discussing a number of general problems raised by the phonological comparison of the East Cushitic languages, 23 consonants are reconstructed for the inventory of the proto-language and the evidence for the reconstructions is presented in the form of cognate sets and correspondence rules which map the proto-phonemes onto the individual reflexes. The method employed is that of comparative linguistics as traditionally employed in Indo-European linguistics.

## TABLE OF CONTENTS

# 1. INTRODUCTORY REMARKS

The following is a preliminary account of what has been done up to now in the reconstruct
of the PEC consonant system. It leaves a good many questions unanswered, and quite a lot
of others totally untouched. I felt, however, that the increasing interest in East
Cushitic languages necessitated a comparative study which could serve both as a reference
point and as a basis for more subtle work along the same lines. I thus decided to publis
a résumé of some seven years of comparative work on East Cushitic. This is the first par
dealing with the consonant system.

Until very recently, progress in comparative Cushitic was hampered by a number of serious
impediments. First of all, very little reliable descriptive material on Cushitic languag
had been printed. The situation was repeatedly outlined by various authors (Palmer (1970
Zaborski (1970, 1976), Sasse (1974)) and need not be discussed here. Suffice it to say
that of the 25 EC languages recognized here only four (Saho-Afar, Somali, Galla and Sidam
were represented by anything like extensive grammars. Secondly, no clear opinion was
current among specialists concerning the nature of the internal relationship of Cushitic:

> "Although we know that some languages must be related, we don't know HOW
> they are related." (Andrzejewski)

> "I wish that our colleagues in the field of Cushitic languages could really
> tell us what is a Cushitic language. So far we don't know." (Leslau)

> "It would be a very great event ... if one day we had something like a
> Common Cushitic or a Common Chadic .... I feel, however, that that happy
> day will never come—not as the result of any lack of will on the part of
> the scholars but due to the very nature of the material." (Garbini)

Quotations from: General Discussion,
Hamito-Semitic Colloquium, London 1970
(Bynon and Bynon (1975:488-9))

Thirdly, the applicability of an exact philological comparative methodology by Indo-European standards has been questioned by several authors for one reason or another (misbelief, linguistic misconceptions, misunderstandings, etc.). This is to some extent understandable, because Cushitists had so often been disappointed by unscientific distortions of the comparative method in their field that they began to deny the possibility of reconstructing exact proto-forms altogether. Some may find it difficult to free their minds of these prejudices, but it is a necessary first step in the direction of a new era in comparative Cushitic. Fortunately, this first step has already been taken. The amount of descriptive material is constantly increasing and the methodological difficulties seem to be decreasing.

The new era made its appearance with Paul Black's excellent dissertation "Lowland East Cushitic" (1974), a work highly compatible and in some respects nearly isomorphic with the present article. Our theoretical frameworks are essentially the same, namely, a solid method of comparative reconstruction similar to that described in recent handbooks such as Anttilla's (1972). There are insignificant areas of disagreement, mainly due to differences in the material (I have extensive data from a considerable number of languages unknown by 1973). In some cases I accepted Black's version, as I found it corroborated by the evidence he presents; in other cases, I prefer my own solutions. Nevertheless, our solutions are always translatable into each other, so that, for the first time in the history of comparative Cushitic, one of the prerequisites of good comparative work seems to be fulfilled. This means that we are both on the right track.

In the meantime others have come to join us. Grover Hudson is currently working on comparative Highland East Cushitic (the former "Burji-Sidamo group"), and Richard Hayward (London) and R. Sim (Nairobi) are treating East Cushitic as a whole. Unfortunately, I have not yet seen any of their results. The last one to join us was Bernd Heine with his recent comparative study of Somali, Boni, and Rendille (1978b), the first comparative study of a well-defined sub-group within East Cushitic.

## 2. EAST CUSHITIC LANGUAGES AND SOURCES OF MATERIAL

The term PEC designates the ancestor language of the following modern languages, language groups, or dialect clusters:

1. Saho-Afar (dialect cluster).

2. Omo-Tana (language group, consisting of a western sub-group (Dasenech, Arbore, Elmolo), an eastern sub-group (Somali, Rendille, Boni) and a northern sub-group (Baiso). The term Omo-Tana, meaning the languages that are spoken in the vast area between the Omo and Tana rivers, was introduced by Heine to replace the formerly used "Macro-Somali" or "Somaloid". For discussion of this group see Heine (1973, 1976, and 1978b) and Sasse (forthcoming)).

3. Macro-Oromo or Oromoid (language group, consisting of the Galla (Oromo) dialects including Waata, and the Konso-Gidole group).

4. The Sidamo group (language group, consisting of Sidamo, Darasa, Alaba, Kambata, Hadiyya/Libido and some others).

5. Burji (language; formerly classified with the Sidamo group. For the separate status of Burji see Sasse and Straube (1977)).

6. Dullay (dialect cluster, consisting of Gawwada, Gollango, Dobase, Harso, Tsamay

and some others; formerly called "Werizoid". For the motivation of the term Dullay see Amborn, Minker, and Sasse (forthcoming)).

    7. Yaaku (Mogogodo; language).

For recent classifications see Black (1972, 1974) and Bender (1971, 1976) where the following terms are used: Highland East Cushitic (HEC) for the Burji-Sidamo group, Lowland East Cushitic (LEC) for the remainder, Somaloid for Heine's (and my) Omo-Tana, Konsoid for my Konso-Gidole, Werizoid for my Dullay. Although the present study does not deal with classification as such, it may be noted that a subclassification of EC is intend which treats the seven above-mentioned groups as more or less equivalent, i.e. a larger group comprising Saho-Afar, Omo-Tana, and Oromoid in the sense of Bender's LEC is not recognized here. This is done because comparative work up to now has not been able to dem onstrate the necessity of reconstructing any intermediate stages between the seven sub-groups and PEC (with one possible exception: Yaaku and Dullay MAY eventually constitute a single sub-group, but this requires further examination).

The sources of the material used for comparison in this paper are as follows. The only modern source of Saho data available to me was Welmers (1952). Afar words are mainly taken from Bliese (1967); in addition, Mahaffy (undated) and Luc (1967) were used. Some-times cognates were only found in Reinisch (1887) on Afar, (1890) on Saho; these are specifically marked. With some citations from older sources, I have taken the liberty of normalizing the orthography. The Somali data are almost exclusively from Abraham (1962) and Bell (1953). The only source of Rendille material is still Heine (1976). For Boni, Heine (1978a) was used. Boni and Rendille data collected by myself a couple of months ago came too late to be included. All Dasenech data stem from my own collection which was made in Ethiopia in 1971/72. The only source of Elmolo data is Heine (1973, 1977). Arbor still remains undescribed; the Arbore data used here are from the collection of Linton, Coolidge and Kaley (undated) collected about 1965; they are phonologically unreliable but unfortunately constitute the only extensive word-list we have. A Baiso word-list has been published by Fleming (1964); in a few cases cognates have been drawn from this list. The Galla material used is mostly from the Borana dialect (own material supplemented by words taken from Andrzejewski's publications); in addition to this, da Thiene's dictionary was used for a number of otherwise unattested words. Konso and Gidole data are again mainly m own, supplemented by a number of words taken from Paul Black's manuscript dictionaries. Moreno's and Cerulli's publications have been used throughout for HEC material (on Sidamo, Moreno (1940), Darasa, Cerulli (1938)), except for Hadiyya, for which Plazikowski-Brauner (1964) provides the most reliable source. My source of Burji data was a still unpublished word-list collected by Straube in 1973 (cf. Sasse and Straube (1977)). The Dullay data were collected by H. Amborn and G. Minker in 1973/74 and analyzed by myself (cf. Amborn, Minker, and Sasse (forthcoming)). Yaaku data are taken from the only available source, Heine (1974).

Special thanks are due to Paul Black, with whom I had a number of fruitful discussions and who provided me with copies of his unpublished Konso and Gidole dictionaries and a cop of his dissertation. I also owe a great deal to Bernd Heine who always showed great gener osity in providing me with his unpublished materials. I also want to express my deep gratitude to the Deutsche Forschungsgemeinschaft without whose financial support during various stages of field research this work would not have been possible.

### 3. THE CONSONANT INVENTORY OF PEC AND SOME GENERAL PROBLEMS

.1.  THE CONSONANT INVENTORY

At the present state of our knowledge, we are able to reconstruct the following consonants (non-syllabic segments) for PEC:

. Plain stops:  voiceless          *t*      *k*      *ʾ*

                voiced        *b*    *d*      *g*

. Glottalized stops:               *d'*     *d'*₁    *k'*

. Fricatives:   voiceless      *ɓ*    *s*    *š*  (*x?*)        *h*    *ħ*

                voiced              *z*                              *ᶜ*

. Liquids and Nasals:          *m*    *n*

                                      *l*

                                      *r*

. Semivowels:                  *w*          *y*

he evidence for the reconstruction of these consonants will be presented in 4.

.2.  VOWELS AND PROSODY

efore discussing some general trends in the historical development of the EC sound system, few remarks on vowels and prosody may be in order.

assume the following vowel system for PEC:

ive short vowels:          *i*      *e*      *a*      *o*      *u*

ive long vowels:          *ii*     *ee*     *aa*     *oo*     *uu*

ne of the greatest problems of PEC vowels is their relative instability.  The minority of he PEC roots can be reconstructed with a stable vowel throughout such as *\*math-* 'head', *malh-* 'pus', or *\*ʾil-* 'eye'.  In the majority of roots, variation is found, as between /u and e/o (the most common type): *\*gilb-/\*gulb-* 'knee', *\*ʾil-/\*ʾul-* 'stick', *\*ᶜils-/ \*ᶜuls-* 'heavy', *\*seg-/\*sog-* 'far', etc., or between a/i/u: *\*lak-/\*lik-/\*luk-* 'foot'; or etween more than three vowels (a/e/i/u as in *\*sar-/\*ser-/\*sir-/\*sur-* 'relative', /i/o/u as in *\*san-/\*sin-/\*son-/\*sun-* 'nose').  Less common combinations appear to be /o/u as in *\*kir-/\*kor-/\*kur-* 'circular formation', e/u(i) as in *\*k'er-/\*k'u(u)r-* 'cut', etc.

ince it is impossible to account for the variation of root vowels in terms of rules operating in individual languages, it is assumed here that "ablaut" played a functional role in PEC.  There is some independent motivation for this assumption:  ablaut still occurs in he prefix conjugation in those languages that preserve prefix verbs (namely, Saho-Afar, somali, Rendille, Boni, Dasenech, Elmolo) as an aspect marker and a derivational device. ore on prefix verbs below.

o the best of my knowledge, all EC languages described so far are tone languages.  Most f them have a relatively simple tonological system which consists of two distinctive units, igh and neutral (in binary terms, ±high).  Tone is seldom used to distinguish roots; its ain function is to mark grammatical categories or to assist segmental morphs in marking such categories (cf., for example, Andrzejewski (1970) on Borana, Mahaffy (undated) on Afar, Sasse (1974) on Dasenech, Heine (1976) on Rendille, etc.). Since this paper is concerned with the reconstruction of roots, tone is not taken into account and is therefor left unmarked throughout.

## 3.3. THE SHAPE OF THE PEC ROOT

The shape of the root is rather uniform in all EC languages. The following general princi ples of PEC word structure can be deduced from the daughter languages with some degree of certainty:

1.  Each root began with one and only one consonant (on initial ꜣ cf. 4.2.1).

2.  No (or very few) words ended in a consonant, i.e. all inflectional morphemes con sisted of or ended in vowels; the naked root did not occur in actual utterances, except possibly in close-knit combinations (or sentence internally in allegro speech). This is approximately the situation still found in Galla, Konso, and other representatives of the Macro-Oromo group, in Dullay, and in all languages of the Sidamo (HEC) group. In the othe languages, final short vowels were generally dropped.

3.  There were no CCC clusters and possibly some rigorous restrictions on CC cluster

4.  The following root shapes mainly occurred:

CV(C), CVCCVC, CVCC, CVCVC.

5.  In addition to the root shapes under 4., PEC had a considerable number of verbs with a discontinuous consonantal root of a Semitic type (prefix verbs): C-C or C-C-C (e.g ꜥ-g 'to drink' or ꜥ-l-ɬ 'to be heavy') from which stems (inflectional bases) were derived by means of fixed vocalic patterns (e.g. verbal adjective of the pattern Ci/uCC: *ꜥilɬ-/ *ꜥulɬ- 'heavy'). It may be assumed that this type of inflection was at one time more widespread, and that some alternants of PEC roots may indeed reflect different 'nominal bases', i.e. different derivations of the same consonantal root. A case in point is *hawl-/*hauwaal- '(1) bury, (2) grave', which may be different derivations from the same consonantal root h-w-l.

According to these principles of root structure, in determining the reflexes of PEC con sonants, we have to examine initial position, medial position, and behavior in CC clusters It has to be borne in mind that the position of one and the same consonant may vary from language to language according to which pattern is represented in the respective word. Th word for 'knee' is represented in two variants, *gilb- and *gulb-. Palatalization takes place in the first variant in Galla and Somali (Galla jilb-a, Somali jilib). In the case of 'bee', however, which is PEC *kann-/kinn-, only Somali has palatalization (shinn-i), whereas Galla originally had the a-variant (kann-iis-a), of course unpalatalized. In the Borana dialect a was assimilated to the ii of the following syllable (kinn-iis-a) after palatalization as a regular sound change had ceased to operate.

## 3.4. DEGEMINATION AND FLUCTUATION IN VOWEL AND CONSONANT LENGTH

All consonants can occur in geminate clusters in Konso and Gidole, and all consonants except h and ꜣ can so occur in Dullay. In Galla, all consonants except ꜣ, h and ny can occur geminated, but gemination is not very stable (Andrzejewski, personal communication). Nevertheless, it appears to be contrastive in numerous minimal pairs and its functional value was confirmed to me by informants from various dialectal areas. These languages thus provide a fairly good starting-point for the reconstruction of PEC geminates. In all

the other EC languages, restrictions on the occurrence of geminates have been introduced.
There is only one case of total degemination (Yaaku).  In Boni and Rendille gemination is
relatively rare and restricted to a small number of consonants.  In Somali, all consonants
are degeminated in final position; intervocalically, however, geminated sonorants (*l, r,
m, n*) and voiced stops (*b, d, g, d*) are permitted and seem to continue the respective PEC
geminates.  *ww* and *yy* are problematic.  Whereas Abraham regularly transcribes intervocalic
semivowels as doubled (with very few exceptions, all after long vowels), Andrzejewski and
Bell do not write double semivowels at all.  On the other hand, Andrzejewski distinguishes
two kinds of *y* (*y* and *y̆*) which do not, however, contrast and thus seem to be allophones
of the same phoneme.  I am thus inclined to believe that Abraham's *ww* and *yy* are an orthographic device to represent tense intervocalic allophones of *w* and *y* and cannot therefore
be taken to support any reconstruction of PEC *\*ww* and *\*yy*.  There is, however, some indication that ALL intervocalic *w*'s in Somali represent *\*ww*, since intervocalic single *\*w*
became Somali *b* (for a more extensive discussion of these problems cf. the chapter on
semivowels, 4.19).  Voiceless stops, fricatives, pharyngeals, laryngeals, and *q* never appear
in geminate clusters in Somali.  For the voiceless stops, degemination is still morphophonemic (/tt/ and /kk/ yield *t* and *k* respectively) and thus intervocalic *t* and *k* can be
taken to continue PEC *\*tt* and *\*kk* when necessary, since single intervocalic *\*t* and *\*k* yield
Somali *d* and *g*.  On degemination as a morphophonemic rule in Dasenech see Sasse (1976).  In
the Sidamo group things are quite chaotic, perhaps because of transcription inadequacies
in the various sources.

According to the evidence just presented, it can be assumed that all consonants could occur
in geminate clusters in PEC, in fact it seems that lengthening of both consonants and
vowels played an important morphophonemic role.  Gemination of the stem-final consonant
was an important means of PEC plural formation which is still operative in Somali (cf.
Abraham (1962:264)), Konso-Gidole (cf. Black (1973:20)), Dasenech (cf. Sasse (1974:415)),
Rendille (cf. Heine (1976:195)), Dullay (cf. Amborn, Minker, and Sasse (forthcoming)),
and to some extent in the Sidamo languages (cf., Plazikowski-Brauner (1960:43) on Hadiyya,
for example).  Other languages preserve some obvious traces of this process.  Gemination
also seems to have occurred before the feminine ending *\*-ee*, cf. Borana *simp'ir-r-e'* 'bird'
vs. Northern Galla *šimbir-a*, Somali *shimbir* etc., and many similar cases, and perhaps before
some other morphemes, e.g. the denominative verbalizing morpheme *\*-a(a)w-* and its causative
*\*-ayš-*.  Furthermore, gemination of stem-final consonants is a derivational marker of the
so-called "singulative verbs" in Konso-Gidole and Dullay (e.g. Konso *ik-k-* 'take a drink'
from *ik-* 'drink'), of which other languages such as Dasenech have preserved traces and
which can therefore be taken to date back to PEC.  In Dasenech and Elmolo, vowel and consonant length in verbs is a morpheme denoting imperfective aspect; this phenomenon, too,
may date back to PEC because it is a characteristic of prefix verbs (the most archaic verb
class) in a number of languages (e.g. Boni imperf. *-iraad-* vs. perf. *-irid-* 'run').  Various
kinds of reduplication, including gemination, are used in intensive, frequentative, and
distributive formation in both verbs and adjectives (this explains root variants such as
*\*bald'-/*\*ballaad'-* 'broad', as already noted by Black (1974)).

Because of extensive analogical levelling, an extraordinary fluctuability of the feature
of length in both vowels and consonants can be observed, and it is clear that the
original shape of many roots has been distorted to a considerable degree.  Roots are
therefore often cited in various alternative shapes; it is left to future research to
determine the original shape for each single case.

## 3.5.  EPENTHETIC VOWELS

EC languages use various devices in order to avoid illicit consonant clusters, the most
obvious of which is vowel epenthesis.  Three different rules of vowel epenthesis can be
reconstructed for PEC:

1. echo-vowel epenthesis (Black calls it "like-vowel epenthesis"), that is, insertion of a vowel that copies the quality of the preceding vowel (e.g. *matħ- → *mataħ-).

2. *i*-insertion (e.g. Dullay /sarp+ti/ → sarp-iti).

3. *a*-insertion (e.g. *ɠur-m- → *ɠur-am-).

Echo-vowel epenthesis operates in some languages (esp. those of the Omo-Tana-group) as a synchronic morphophonemic rule; it is less widespread in the languages of the Dullay and Oromoid groups; nevertheless vestiges can be found in all EC languages. *i*-insertion is virtually absent in Somali and Rendille but occurs in other languages of the Omo-Tana group. It is the normal mode of cluster-resolution in Dullay, and competes with—but seem to be preferred to—echo-vowel epenthesis in Boni and Galla. In Dasenech, the distribution of echo-vowel epenthesis and *i*-insertion seems to be governed by the absence or presence of a morpheme boundary inside the cluster to be mitigated (see Sasse (1976)).

*a*-insertion is most wide-spread in the Oromoid languages (Konso ikas- : iššš- 'kill', poqaɫ poqɫ- 'king'; Galla dubar- : dubr- 'girl'). It is also found in the Omo-Tana languages, but restricted to the verb derivatives -m- 'passive' and -t- 'middle voice' : Som. ɠur-m-a ɠur-am-ta.

Galla and perhaps other Oromoid languages further complicate the situation in that they seem to have elided *i* in open syllables (Galla bakaɫc-a 'Venus' < *bakkaɫ-it-a, Konso oxn-aa 'fences', sg. oxin-ta).

The overall similarities suggest that all three mechanisms of vowel insertion were already operating in PEC before the split into the individual languages; their exact distribution, however, still remains to be reconstructed. Since this situation complicates the reconstruction of CVCC patterns, all roots which have the structure $CV_iCV_iC$ in languages with echo-vowel epenthesis are generally reconstructed as CVCC roots (provided that comparative or internal evidence can be adduced for such a reconstruction, otherwise they are tentatively set up as CVCVC until further arguments are found to support a different reconstruction). For a detailed discussion of echo-vowel epenthesis see Black (1974:143ff.).

## 3.6.  PALATALIZATION

Palatalization is common in Somali, Rendille, Boni, Dasenech, Galla, Burji and Yaaku. The consonants involved are PEC *k, *g, *k', t, and $*d'_1$, when preceding (in the case of t also following) front vowels.

As demonstrated by Heine (1978b), palatalization of *k and *g appears to be among the clearest phonological evidence for positing a Somali-Rendille-Boni subgroup within Omo-Tana. Before the split of the common ancestor of these languages, PEC *k had already become *c in the palatalizing contexts, and it continues as Somali and Boni š (y intervocalically) and as Rendille c. Similarly, PEC *g in palatalizing contexts became *j, which continues as Somali and Rendille j, but merged with Boni š to yield š as a result of the general devoicing of obstruents. Some common cases of irregular palatalization (e.g. *cub- 'to pour' from PEC *kub-) further strengthen the assumption of a common source for palatalization in Somali, Boni, and Rendille. The remainder of the Omo-Tana group, on the other hand, shows only slight signs of palatalization. Dasenech palatalizes k before e and t before *i* into c; there are fewer than a handful of irregular palatalizations in Arbore and Elmolo, probably diffused through dialect borrowing, from Dasenech or a similar dialect. Baiso does not palatalize at all.

Somali went a step further in that it also palatalizes *k' (normally → Som. q) into j. Palatalization of both g and q is still morphophonemic in Somali, e.g. before the causativ suffix: *nuug-* 'suck': caus. *nuuj-i-*, *baq-* 'be afraid': caus. *baj-i-*. Palatalization of the velars also occurs in Galla; it is certainly (genetically) independent of Somali, although it shows very similar results.  *k* becomes *ǯ* which further shifts to *ž* in certain dialects, *g* becomes *j*, and *k'* becomes *c'*. There is no trace of a morphophonemic alternation.  Unlike Somali, Galla also palatalizes *t* to *ž* after *i*.

The only palatalizing languages outside the "Lowland East Cushitic" core are Burji and Yaaku.  Burji is phonologically very similar to Galla, the palatalization reflexes being identical with those of Galla, viz. *k → ž, g → j, k' → c'*.  In addition to the velars, *t* becomes *c* initially and *ǯ* medially in the palatalizing environments.  Palatalization in Yaaku is totally different from that of other EC languages and will be treated in connection with other problems of the historical phonology of Yaaku in Appendix A.  It has already been stated that, to the exclusion of Somali-Rendille-Boni, palatalization has to be regarded as an independent development in each language.  This can be adduced from the fact that there is little agreement among the individual languages as to the roots which undergo palatalization, since root vowels may differ in frontness.  Cf., e.g., PEC *\*kir-/\*kur-* 'a round, a circular formation', which yields Konso *kur-eta* 'circular dance' and Galla *kor-a* 'assembly', but Somali *shir* 'assembly, conference, meeting, council'; or Somali *shaley(to)* 'yesterday' as against Galla *kalee-sa*. This latter difference is due to an irregular development of PEC *\*kal-* 'yesterday' (cf. also Konso *xal-a*, Gidole *hal-a*, and Yaaku *xaal-in*) into Proto-Omo-Tana *\*kel-* (perhaps by vowel assimilation, *\*kal-ay → \*kel-ey-*? Cf. Rendille *cele*, Boni *ǯaleᵉ, ǯeleᵉ'*, Elmolo *ele'* (with irregular loss of *k*), and Baiso *kele*).

Despite this individuality of development, it is not unlikely that palatalization constitutes an areal phenomenon spread by diffusion rather than an independent innovation in each language.  Its source may have been Eastern Omo-Tana, which must at any rate have been in close contact with Proto-Galla.  The latter, after taking it over from Omo-Tana, carried it on to Burji, which is probably the youngest of the palatalizaing languages.

## 3.7.  SOUND CHANGES AFFECTING VOICE

In Somali, voiceless plosives in postvocalic position merged with their voiced counterparts. The geminates *tt*, *kk* retain their voiceless articulation, but are degeminated to *t* and *k*, respectively.  Consequently, Som. postvocalic *d*, *g* are not representative of PEC *\*d*, *\*g*, unless their voiced character is confirmed by other languages.  For examples cf. 4.1 and 4.2; on voicing as a morphophonemic rule in Somali cf. Bell (1953:8-9) and Abraham (1962: 268 etc.).  Boni seems to have had a very similar rule.

Konso-Gidole and a large number of the Dullay dialects share a phenomenon of devoicing of the voiced plosives, partly paralleled by spirantization of voiceless plosives.  In particular, the following sound changes have taken place in these languages:

| PEC | Konso | Gidole | Harso-Dobase | Gollango |
|-----|-------|--------|--------------|----------|
| *\*t* | *t* | *ǯ,t* | *c,t* | *t* |
| *\*k* | *x,k* | *h* | *h* | *x* |
| *\*b* | *p* | *p* | *p* | *p* |
| *\*d* | *t* | *t* | *t* | *t* |
| *\*g* | *k* | *k* | *k* | *k* |

On the areal character of these changes see Black (1975) and Amborn, Minker and Sasse (forthcoming).

Similar devoicing processes are found in other EC languages, viz. Elmolo, Boni and Yaaku.
On the latter see Appendix A.  In Elmolo and Boni devoicing does not affect the whole
system; Elmolo changes *b* to *p* and some instances of *d* to *t*, while others remain unchanged,
and Boni regularly changes initial *d* and *g* to *t* and *k*, respectively, but retains *b*.  On
the other hand, medial *t* and *k* had been changed to *d* and *g* in a previous stage of Boni,
and there is doubtlessly a causal connection between these two sound changes.

#### 4. EVIDENCE FOR THE INDIVIDUAL CONSONANT PHONEMES

4.1.  PEC *t*

There is a series of correspondences which can be easily accounted for by the reconstruction of a voiceless plain coronal stop symbolized as *t*.  It occurs in all possible
positions and displays the following individual reflexes:  Saho and Afar *t*; Somali *t* except in the positions indicated in 3.7 where it becomes voiced *d*; Rendille *t*; Baiso *t*;
Arbore *t*; Dasenech *t* initially and finally, *z* intervocalically; Elmolo *t* (realized as *d* or
*ð* intervocalically); Boni *t* initially, *d* (realized as *ð*) non-initially; Galla *s* after *i*
and *y*, *t* elsewhere; Konso *t*; Gidole *s* and *t*; HEC *t*; Burji *t*; Yaaku *t*.  The reflexes in
the Dullay languages are determined by an isogloss separating those dialects that display
a *t*-reflex from those that display a *c*-reflex.  This isogloss is not consistent with any
one of the larger units recognized here, but at least the whole Harso dialect belongs
to the *c*-group, whereas the whole Gollango dialect belongs to the *t*-group.

For some individual peculiarities see below.

Examples of initial *t*:

*\*tuɓ-* 'spit': Saho-Afar *tuɓ-*; Somali *tuɓ-*, Arbore *tuɓ-*; Galla *tuɓ-*, Konso *tuɓ-*, Gidole
*šuh-*; HEC *tuɓ-*; Burji *tuɓ-*; Dullay *tuɓ-* and *cuɓ-* depending on the dialect.

*\*tom(m)an-/\*tomn-* 'ten': Som. *toban*, Bai. *tomon ~ toman*, Rend. *tomon*, Arb. *tomon*, Das.
*tommon*, Elm. *tomon*, Boni *taman*; Galla *\*-tama ~ \*-toma* as in *soddoma* 'thirty', *afurtama*
'fourty'; Sidamo *tonn-e* (< *tomn-e*), Darasa *tomn-e*, Kambata *ton-a*, Alaba *tomn-o*, Hadiyya
*tom-o*; Burji *tann-a*.  The dialectal distribution of the following Saho and Afar reflexes
is not entirely clear:  Saho *tamman*, *tomon*, Afar *toban*, *taban*.

*\*tum-* 'pound, beat, forge': Afar *tum-* 'crush'; Som. *tum-*, Rend. *tum-*, Das. *tun-*, Boni
*tum-a* (< *tum-aal*) 'blacksmith'; Galla *tum-*, Konso *tum-*, Gidole *šum-*; Yaaku *tuµ²-*.

Examples of medial *t*:

*\*k'ot-* 'dig': Som. *qod-*, Rend. *xut-*, Boni *od-*, Arbore *kot-* 'plow', Das. *g'ot/z-* 'dig,
bury'; Ga. *k'ot-*, Kon. *qot-*, Gid. *k'oš-*; Gawwada *qot-*.

*\*²at-* 'thou': Saho-Afar *at-u*; Somali *adi(-ga)*, Baiso *ati*, Rend. *ati*, Boni *adi*; Galla *ati*,
Konso *at-ti* (i.e. *at-* + subject case ending), Gidole *at-te* (*at-* + subject case ending);
HEC *ati*; Dullay *ato* and *aco* depending on the dialect.  On Burji *aši* see below.

*\*gat-* 'sell': Som. (dial.) *gad-*, Rend. *gat-* 'buy, sell', Boni *kad-*; Galla *gat-* 'throw
away, (dial.) sell', Konso *kat-*, Gid. *kaš-*; HEC *gat-*; Burji *gat-*.

*\*math-* 'head': Som. *madah*, Baiso *mete* (cf. 4.17), Rend. *matah*, Boni *mada'*, Arbore *mete*,
Das *me* (irregular loss of *t*; cf. pl. *mett-u*), Elmolo *mete²*; Galla *mataa*, Konso *matta*, Gid.
*mašš(a)*; Yaaku *miteh*.

Individual phonologically conditioned deviations from these normal reflexes are found in some languages. According to the morpheme-structure rules of Galla, which forbid sequences of voiced and voiceless stops, *t* becomes *d* after a voiced stop. It appears furthermore that Galla has an *š* reflex of *t* after *i* and *y* (cf. Sasse (1975)), as in the singulative suffix *-ita*, *-yta* (*d'iir-ita* 'husband' → *d'iir-ša*, *gelz-a-yta* 'baboon' → *jald-eeša*). Perhaps also *isini*, *isani* 'you' (pl.) may be explained in this way (PEC *\*ᵓatin-* or *\*ᵓitin-*). Burji also seems to have *š* and *c* reflexes of *t* in certain environments (cf. Sasse and Straube (1977)). In addition, Burji changes *t* to *š* before *i*, and the latter is often lost subsequently, cf. *aš(i)* 'thou'. In Dasenech, *t* followed by *i* sometimes occurs as *c*, as in *cira* 'liver' (PEC *\*tir-* as reconstructed from Saho-Afar *tir-o*, Galla *tir-uu*, Gidole *šir-a*, Dullay *cir-e* etc.).

A minor problem involves the conditioning of the Gidole reflexes *š* and *t* which appears to have been obscured by analogical levelling. Whereas *š* always represents *t* in initial position, there is no way to predict under what circumstances PEC *\*t* becomes Gid. *š* or *t* medially. Examples for Gid. *t* from PEC *\*t* include the personal endings for 2s, 3sf and 2p (*-tV* and *-tVnV*, respectively), and the singulative suffix *-ta*. Since both sets of suffixes are added primarily to stems ending in consonants, the original distribution of the *t* and *š* reflexes of *\*t* may perhaps have been conditioned by the types of segments that preceded the *\*t* prior to the change.

I was not able to reconstruct any PEC root containing geminate *tt*. On the evidence at hand it may be expected that *\*tt* should continue as Somali *t* (as morphophonemic /tt/ actually does), as Macro-Oromo *tt* (perhaps subject to optional degemination in Galla), as Dasenech *tt*, Dullay *tt/cc*, and Yaaku *t*.

## 4.2.  PEC *\*k*

For palatalization of *\*k* see 4.3. In non-palatalizing contexts, PEC *\*k* yields the following reflexes: Saho-Afar *k*; Proto-Omo-Tana *\*k* continuing as Somali *k* (*g* after vowels according to 3.7), Baiso *k*, Rendille *h* word-finally, *k* elsewhere, Arbore *k*, Dasenech and Elmolo *k* initially and finally Ø elsewhere, Boni *k*; Galla *k*; Konso *k* initially before front vowels and *u*, *x* elsewhere; Gidole *h*; HEC *k* (possibly Sidamo *h* after vowels in some cases? see below); Burji *k*; Dullay *k* after consonants except when separated from them by a morpheme boundary,[1] *h* and *x* depending on the dialect elsewhere, Yaaku *k* (but possibly also *x* in some cases).

Examples of initial *\*k*:

*\*kuɓ-* 'fall' (secondarily 'die' in some languages): Som. *kuɓ-*, Rend. *kuɓ-*, Arb. *kuɓ-*, Das. *kuɓ-* 'die', Elm. *kuɓ-*, Boni *kuɓ-*; Galla *kuɓ-*; Yaaku *kup-* 'die'.

*\*kool-* 'feather, wing': Boni *koolᵘ* 'wing'; Das. *kuol*, Elm. *kool'* 'shoulder'; Galla *kool-a*, Konso *xool-a*; Burji *kool-i*; Gawwada *xool-akko*, Harso *hool-o*, Gollango *xool-o*; Yaaku *kol* 'branch'.

*\*kaᶜ-* 'wake up, get up': Som. *kaᶜ-*, Boni *kiᵓ-i'* (caus.) 'wake up', Das. *keᵓ-*, Elm. *keᵓ-* 'go away', *ke-is-* (caus.) 'raise'; Galla *kaᵓ-*, Konso *xa-*, Gid. *haᵓ-*; Sidamo *kaᵓ-* 'get up, go away', Darasa *ke-*, Alaba *ki-*, Hadiyya *kiᵓ-*; Burji *kaᵓ-*; Gawwada *xaᶜ-* 'fly',

---

[1] Thus Harso *hisk-e* 'star' < PEC *\*hizk-*, but *\*halhal+ko* 'beard' yields *halhal-ho*. Sometimes the voiced allophone of *k* has been phonemicized and is now assigned to a new phoneme /g/ with voiced and occasionally slightly implosive allophones, as in Harso *ilg-akko* 'tooth'.

Harso *hac-*; Yaaku *kɛʔɛ* 'plant, put up'.[2]

Examples of medial *k:

*lak-/*lik-/*luk-* 'foot, leg': Saho-Afar *lak*; Som. *lug*, Baiso *lukk-a*,[3] Rend. *luħ*, Arb. *luk-a*, Elm. *luk*; Galla *luk-a* 'thigh', Gid. *lukk-et* (dial. *luh-e*); Sid. *lekk-a*, Dar. *lekk-a*, Kamb. *lokk-o*, Alaba *lokk-a*, Had. *lokk-o*; Gaw. *lux-te*, Harso *luh-te*. Konso has irregular *loq-ta*.

*ʔilk-* tooth': Saho *ik-o*; Som. *ilig* (pl. *ilk-o*), Rend. *ilaħ* (pl. *ilk-o*), Boni *ilk-e* (pl.), Baiso *ilk-o* (prob. pl.), Arbore *ilk-wa* (prob. pl.), Elm. *ilk-o'* ('teeth'); Galla *ilk-aani* (pl.), Konso *ilk-itta*, Gidole *ilh-itt* (dial. *ilh-a*); Gaw. *ilg-e*, Harso *ilg-akko*. The HEC, Burji, and Yaaku cognates show irregular correspondences: Burji *irk'-a*, Sid. *hink-o*, Kamb. *ink-e*, Alaba *ink'-u*, Had. *ink'-ee*, and Yaaku *inj-e-ni*, pl. *inj-e'*.

Examples for PEC -*kk*- are:

*lakk-* 'both, twin': Galla *lakk-uu* 'twin' (also *lacc-uu* 'both', probably < *lak-šuu*), Konso *lakk-i* 'two', Gidole *lakk-e* 'two'; Dullay *lakk-i* 'two'.

*lukk-* 'chicken': Rend. *luk-u*, Baiso *luk-ale*, Das. *lug*, pl. *lugg-u*,[4] Galla *lukk-uu*, Konso *lukk-al-itta*, Gid. *lukk-al-itt*; Sid. *lukk-icco*, Dar. *lukk-o*; Burji *lukk-ano*; Gaw. *lukk-akko*, Harso *lukk-al-akko*.

Examples of the Konso reflexes of *k:

Before *o*: *xop-ta* 'sandal' (PEC *kob-*, cf. Galla *kop'-ee* ~ *kob-ee*).

Before *a*: *xal-l-àa* 'kidney' (PEC *kal-*, cf. Som. *kel-l-i*, Galla *kal-ee*).

Before *e*: *ken* 'five' (PEC *ken-*, cf. 4.3).

Before *i*: *kirp-* 'dance and sing' (PEC *kirb-*, cf. 4.3).

Before *u*: *kut-a* 'dog' (PEC *kut-*, cf. Afar *kut-a*).

In Sidamo, the regular reflexes of PEC *k seem to have been *h* intervocalically, *k* elsewhere, as suggested by the following etymologies: PEC *kum-* 'thousand' (Galla, Konso, Burji *kum-a*, Somali *kun*) → Sid. *kum-e*; PEC *kebeel-* 'leopard' (cf. 4.3) → *kabeel-co*; PEC *kac-* 'get up' quoted above, as against PEC *zak-* 'swim' (Sasse (1976)) → *dah-*; cf. also the demonstrative *ko* 'this' which becomes -*ho* when employed as a clitic. This original distribution is now largely obscured through analogical leveling. It is possible that in this way *k* was generalized in some roots that originally had a final *h*; so *suk-* 'twist' is probably cognate with PEC *sooh-* 'id.', as attested in Som., Boni, Ko., Gid. *sooh-*, Galla *fooh-*, Rend. *soh-* 'twist, plait', but it cannot be excluded that such cases of *h* : *k* correspondences reflect a different protophoneme (e.g. *x, cf. 4.10).

---

[2]PEC *kac-* is derived from a former prefix verb *k-c* still represented as such in forms such as Saho -*uy-kuc-/-ay-kac-* (caus.) 'lift, carry'.

[3]The forms showing *kk* are secondary. Lengthening is perhaps a feminine marker (there is evidence for consonant lengthening in femining forms, cf. 3.4).

[4]General devoicing of obstruents in word-final position leads to the ambiguous form [luk] which was reinterpreted as /lug/.

.3.  PALATALIZATION OF *k

he general principles of palatalization in EC were outlined in 3.6.  Palatalization of *k
ook place in Somali, Rendille, Boni, Dasenech, Galla, and Burji; on Yaaku cf. Appendix A.
he palatalized reflexes of *k are Somali š (and y intervocalically), Rendille c, Boni š,
asenech c, Galla š (which is currently in the process of shifting to s in most of the
ialects, cf. Sasse (1975)), and Burji š.  The palatalizing context is a following *e and
i in all languages except Dasenech, where—rather unnaturally—*i seems to be excluded,
. *ken- 'five' → Das. cen, but *kimbir- 'bird' becomes kimir- (sg. kimidd'i, underlying
imir+ti/, pl. kimir-n-i).  On the other hand, there is one example of the cluster *ky
ecoming c, as in -cu 'my' < *k-yu.

: is likely that the Somali, Rendille and Boni reflexes of palatalized *k are not in-
ependent creations but reflect a common ancestor *c which occurred in the common proto-
:age of these three languages (cf. Heine (1978b)), let us call it Proto-Eastern-Omo-Tana
PEOT).  PEOT *c is a merger of the reflexes of palatalized *k and those relics of PEC
i that had not become s in pre-PEOT, cf. 4.16.

me examples of palatalized *k are given below.

C *kebeel- 'leopard', as reconstructed from Sid. kebeel-co, Hadiyya kabeer-a, Yaaku
ᵊpen, yields Somali šabeel, Boni šuweel'.  Rendille has kabil, probably reflecting a
roto-form with different vocalization.[5]

C *ken- 'five', as represented in Baiso ken-i, Elmolo ken, Konso ken, Gidole hen-e,
ields Somali šan, Rendille can, Boni šan, Das. cen, and Galla šan-i.

C *ker- 'dog', as represented in Saho kar-e, Baiso ker-n-e, Arbore kair, ker-e, Elmolo
r-(e), Gidole her-n-a, Dullay xar-o and har-o depending on the dialect, yields Galla
r-ee, and Dasenech cer or cir (fem. cedd'i /cer+ti/ 'bitch').  Rendille kar is clearly
borrowing, the PEOT root for 'dog' being *ᵊey-/*ᵊoy-.

C *kilm- 'tick', as represented in Saho-Afar kilim, yields Somali šilin (pl. šilm-o),
nd. cilim, Boni šilm-i', and Galla šilm-a, šilm-ii, silm-ii according to dialect.

C *kimbir- 'small bird', as represented in Saho kimbir-o, Baiso kimbiri, Dasenech
imidd'i, Arbore kirmate etc., yields Somali šimbir, Rend. cimbir, Boni šimir, and Galla
imbir-a, simbir-a, simp'ir-n-ee according to dialect.

C *kirb- 'dance and sing', as represented in Konso kirp-, Gidole hirp-, Gawwada xirip-,
rso hirp-, yields Somali širb-o 'circular dance', Galla širb-, Burji šibir- (by metathesis).

. also Burji še, Konso ke from PEC *ki (Galla si) 'thee'.

ere is one instance of irregular palatalization of initial *k before *u in PEOT *cub-
omali and Boni šub-) from PEC *kub- (cf. Konso kup-p-) 'pour out'.

ly one example of a palatalized *k in intervocalic position has been found:

ik-ee 'water': Som. biy-o, Rend. bic-e, Boni biy-o', Baiso bek-e, Das. bi-e, Galla
š-aani and bis-aani depending on the dialect.  Elmolo bec-e' ~ bic-i' and Arbore
yc-e show irregular c reflexes.  Konso piš-a must be a loan from Galla.

---

[5]The form *kebeel- itself is an extension of a more basic *kebᶜ-, still represented in
aho-Afar qabeᶜ, qabᶜ-ita, kabᶜ-i or the like, Baiso kebɪh, and Yaaku çeᵊpe', with an
therwise unattested suffix -eel-.

## 4.4.   PEC *b

PEC *b is normally reflected by Saho-Afar b, Somali b, Rendille b, Boni b (with a fricative
allophone β in intervocalic position, sometimes approaching w), Arbore b, Dasenech b
initially and finally as the second member of a cluster, Ø elsewhere, Elmolo p (with
voiced and fricative allophones, sometimes transcribed as b by Heine and hence easy to
confuse with his /b/ = b'), Baiso b; Galla b, Konso and Gidole p (cf. 3.7); HEC b (with
free (?) variants w, β in Sidamo); Burji b; Dullay p (cf. 3.7); and Yaaku p, w and Ø (cf.
Appendix A).

Geminate *bb is retained as pp in Dullay and Konso-Gidole, and as such in HEC, Burji, and
perhaps Saho-Afar; in Somali, Galla, and Dasenech it is optionally degeminated according
to principles yet to be worked out.  In Rendille and Boni *bb occurs as b; the transcrip-
tions of the remainder of the EC languages are not reliable enough to allow any conclusion.

For some individual deviations from these regular reflexes see below.

Examples of initial *b:

*bad- be lost, extinguished': Saho-Afar ba(a)d- 'perish, be extinguished'; Das. bad-, Elm.
pɛd-; Galla bad- 'be lost', Konso pat- 'be ruined', Gidole pat- 'disappear, be lost, die';
Burji bas-ʂ- (caus.) 'extinguish' (< *bad-ʂ-); Gawwada and Harso pat- 'disappear',
Gollango pat- 'get lost'. Probably Somali bad- 'involve in trouble' and bad-baad- 'escape'
also belong here.

*baɾ-ɾ- 'time': Saho baɾ-oy- 'grow old', baɾ-iin 'old', baɾ-a 'old man/woman'; Somali
beɾ-i 'time', Elmolo paɾɾ-ac 'daytime'; Galla baɾ-a 'time, year, age', Konso paɾ-a 'year,
age'; HEC *baɾɾ- (e.g. Sid. baɾɾ-a 'day, time', Had. baʟʟ-a 'day, date'); Burji beɾɾ-i
'year'; Gawwada and Harso peɾ-ko 'year', paɾ-a 'when'.

*biʂ- 'flower, color': Afar biʂ-u 'color'; Galla biɟ-a 'color', Konso piʂ-a 'flower';
Burji biš-a 'color'; Gawwada piʂ-o, Harso and Gollango piʂ-ko 'flower'.

Examples of medial *b:

*k'ab- 'catch, have': Saho kab- (but also ab- 'make, do', ab-it- (middle voice) 'take
for oneself'; Somali qab-, Boni ob-, Elmolo ap- 'touch', Das. g'a(b)-, Arb. kab-;
Galla k'ab-, Konso qap-, Gidole k'ap-; Sidamo ab-ʔid'- 'portare per se, sposare'; Dullay
qap-.  Burji has irregular k'aɟ-.

*malab- 'honey': Saho-Afar mala(a)b-; Somali malab, Rendille malab, Boni malub; Sidamo
and Kambata malab-o, Hadiyya maɾab-o.

*ʔaɾb- 'elephant': Somali aɾb-e (Andrzejewski), Rendille aɾab, Elmolo aɾap, Arbore aɾb-a,
Dasenech ʔaɾab, pl. ʔaɾb-u; Galla aɾb-a, Konso aɾp-a, Gidole aɾp(-a); Burji aɾb-a; Harso
and Gollango aɾap-ko; Yaaku aɾap-e 'large feline' (Ehret), aɾap-a 'carnivorous animal'
(Heine).

In some of the languages a glottalized p' or b' appears as an irregular reflex of *b.
E.g. we have Sidamo gulupp'-o 'knee' vs. Hadiyya guɾubb-o.  I assume that most p' or b'
reflexes can be explained by a hypothesis of secondary glottalization, unless they are
due to borrowing.  This is particularly evident in Galla, where we have at least one clear
case of p' resulting from a fusion of b + ᶜ: nyaap'-a 'enemy' from PEC *neᶜb-.  Similar
explanations will be proposed for Galla ʂup'-ee 'clay' and ʟap'-ee 'breastbone' in 4.21.
Some further occurrences of p' seem to be due to some glottalized element in the same word

e.g. *c'ap'-* 'break' as resulting from *c'ab-* through assimilation of *b* to *c'*. A handful of instances not explainable in this way may perhaps be taken to represent relics of lost morphophonemic alternations (cf. 4.21). In any case, the extreme degree of variation even within single dialects of the same language clearly demonstrates that a glottalized labial cannot be reconstructed for PEC.

In Dasenech and Boni, *b* has a zero reflex after *m, cf. *kimbir- 'bird' → Das. /kimir-/, Boni *šimir*. Boni has, however, *sombob-*[u] 'lungs' (Das. regularly *saam-ic*).

Galla possesses a morphophonemic rule turning *b* to *m* before nasals, cf. /k'ab+na/ 'we have' → *k'amn*[a]. I have found only two dubious cognates showing this reflex: Ga. *humn-aa* 'muscle, power', Konso *hupn-a* 'power, strength, energy', and Somali *hubin* 'limb', which may be reconstructed as PEC *hubn- (original meaning 'muscle'?), and Galla *gamn-aa* 'sly, cunning, fine' perhaps = Som. *gaban, gabin, gibin* 'small', which may reflect a PEC *gabn- with the meaning 'dainty, delicate, neat' or the like.

Final *b → m* in Dasenech in a number of cases, e.g. *gub- 'mountain' → *gum*, *dub- 'tail' → *dum*.

Examples of *bb* include:

*ʾaabb-/*ʾabb- 'father': Saho-Afar *abb-a*; Somali *aabb-e* 'father' and *abb-aan* 'protector', Rend. *ab-a*, Baiso *abb-o*; Galla *abb-aa* 'father (general)', *aabb-oo* 'own father', Konso *aapp-a*, Gidole *app-a*; Hadiyya *aabb-a* (rare); Burji *aabb-o*; Yaaku *paa* (= *p-aa*?).

## 4.5.  PEC *d

As PEC *d and *z have merged into a single *d* (which later became *t* in languages with loss of voice contrast) in most Saho dialects and Afar, Northern Somali, Baiso, Macro-Oromo, HEC (except Alaba), Burji, and Boni, evidence for *d can only come from those languages that have preserved distinct reflexes of both consonants. In these languages we observe the following reflexes of *d and *z:

|                  | *d  | *z     |
|------------------|-----|--------|
| Saho dialects    | d   | z ~ ð  |
| Southern Somali  | d   | y      |
| Rendille         | d   | y      |
| Arbore           | d   | z      |
| Dasenech         | d   | z ~ ð  |
| Elmolo           | t   | y, w   |
| Alaba            | d   | z      |
| Dullay           | t   | s      |
| Yaaku            | t   | s      |

Arbore *z* sometimes appears as *ds, dz* in the sources. This is mainly the case with words where *zz* is expected; I therefore assume that it is an orthographic device used by the authors in order to represent something like a geminate *z*. Both Elmolo and Yaaku *t* have voiced allophones and are hence transcribed as *d* by Heine in some words. Dasenech offers no evidence for *d or *z as a stem-final consonant in verb stems, because in this position *t, d,* and *z* have merged into a single morphophoneme with the exponents *t* or *z* according to the environment.

Examples of PEC *z will be given in 4.9.

Examples of initial *d:

*daⱦᶜ- 'ashes': Galla *daaⱦ-aa*, Konso *taⱦ-a*, Gidole *teⱦᵓ-ata* (Black: *teⱦd'-at*); Burji *daaⱦ-a*; Gawwada, Harso, and Gollango *taⱦᶜ-o*.

*dey-/*doy- 'look at': Somali *day-* 'examine', Boni *day-* 'try, test', Arbore *doy-* 'see', Elmolo *doy-* 'regard'; Galla *doy-aa* 'observation', *dooy-aa* 'spy', Konso and Gidole *tooy-* 'see'; Hadiyya *do-* 'lurk, spy'; Harso *tay-* 'find'; Yaaku *tey-* 'find, get'.

*dib-/*dub- 'back, tail' (also *dibb-/*dubb-): Som. *dib* 'short tail of goat, etc.', Rend. *dub* 'tail', Boni *tib* 'tail', Elm. *dup*, Das. *dum* 'tassel of animal's tail'; Galla *dub-a* and *duub-a* (depending on the dialect) 'behind', Konso *tup-a* 'behind', *tup-p-aa* 'upper back'; Alaba *dubb-o* 'tail', Hadiyya *dubb-o* 'behind'; Gawwada, Harso and Gollango *tup-* (with various extensions) 'behind, after'. Somali *dab-o* and Baiso *deb-e* 'tail' reflect a third vocalization type *dab-.

Examples of medial *d:

*diid- 'refuse': Somali *diid-*, Rendille *diid-*, Boni *tiid-*, Arbore *did-*, Dasenech *diit/z-*; Galla *diid-* (Borana *did-*), Konso *tiit-*.

*god- 'hole in the ground, cave': Somali *god* 'hole in the ground', Rendille *god* 'id.'; Galla *god-a* 'hole, cave'; Hadiyya *god-aᵓa* 'wall'; Burji *god-o* 'trash dump, cesspit'; Dulla *kot-o* 'small hut for cooking', also 'house' in some dialects.[6]

*bidħ-[7] 'left side': Somali *bidiħ*, Boni *bidah*, Arbore *biyde*; Galla *bita-a* (with assimilation of d before *ħ*), Konso *pitt-itta*, Gidole *piht-ot* (by metathesis); Gollango *piħat-e* (by metathesis).

Two roots with geminate *dd have been reconstructed:

*gudd- 'big': Arbore *gud-*, Dasenech *gudd-u*, Elmolo *kut-at-* 'grow old'; Galla *guud-aa*, Konso and Gidole *kutt-*. Somali *gudd* 'top', Dasenech *gudd-an-aya* 'enlarge', and Elmolo *guut-* 'many' reflect a different base *guud-.

*gidd- 'middle': Galla *jidd-uu*; Sidamo *gidd-o* 'inside', Hadiyya *gud-a* (probably a transcription error for *gudd-a*, because *dd* otherwise occurs) 'half, middle'; Harso *kitt-e*, *kitt-o* 'middle'.


4.6.  PEC *g

For palatalization of *g see 3.6 and below. In non-palatalizing contexts, PEC *g shows the following reflexes in the individual languages: Saho-Afar *g*, Somali *g*, Rendille *g*, Boni *k* (cf. 3.7), Baiso *g*, Arbore *g*, Dasenech *g* initially and finally (pronounced [k] word-finally and thus assigned to a phoneme /k/ unless there is alternation with *g*), zero intervocalically, Elmolo *k*,[8] Galla *g*, Konso and Gidole *k* (cf. 3.7), HEC *g*, Burji *g*,

---

[6]The semantic shift 'hole' → 'wall' → 'building' is well motivated by the cultural background, since the construction of underground houses is common in southern Ethiopia. The same shift of meaning is observed in another PEC word for 'hole', *bohl-*, which became Gidole *pohol-aa* 'wall'. On the latter cf. Black (1974:233, fn. 50).

[7]This root was reconstructed as *bith-* in some of my earlier publications. Paul Black has, however, pointed out to me that the Arbore and Gidole forms unambiguously lead to the reconstruction of d.

[8]The conditioning of eventual zero reflexes of *k and *g in Elmolo has yet to be determined. Elmolo /k/ has a voiced allophone medially which is sometimes transcribed as *g* by Heine and thus confused with his /g/ [g'].

ullay *k*[9] (cf. 3.7), and Yaaku *k* (cf. 3.7 and Appendix A).

or some individual peculiarities see below.

xamples of initial *\*g*:

*gan*ᶜ- '(palm of) hand': Saho *gina*ᶜ, Afar *gena*ᶜ-*ta* (probably from *\*gana*ᶜ by vowel dissimi-
ation, as in *miga*ᶜ 'name' from *\*maga*ᶜ (PEC *\*mag*ᶜ-), or else possibly reflecting a
lifferent nominal base); Somali *ga*ᶜ*an* (by metathesis), Boni *ka*ᵓ*an* (by metathesis), Baiso
*ene*; Galla *gana-a* (< *\*gan*ᶜ-*a*), Konso *kan-aata*, Gidole *kana*ᵓ-*at*; Dullay *kana*ᶜ-ᶜ-*e* (pl.);
aaku *kinn*ε*ᵓ*- (cf. Appendix A).

*gal*- 'enter, go home': Somali *gal*- (also *gel*-), Rend. *gel*-, Boni *kal*-; Galla *gal*-, Konso,
;idole *kal*-; HEC *gal*- (Sid., Dar., Kamb. *gal*-, Had. *gaar*-) 'stay overnight'; Burji *gal*-.

*gub*- 'burn': Som. *gub*-, Rend. *gub*-, Boni *kub*-; Galla *gub*-, Konso *kup*-; Yaaku *kup*-'rot'.

xamples of medial *\*g*:

*ᶜag-*/*\*ᶜig-*/*\*ᶜug*- (previously a prefix verb *\*-ᶜag-*/-ᶜig-/-ᶜug-) 'drink': Boni -*a*ᵓ*ak*-/-*i*ᵓ*ik*-
prefix conjugation), Arbore -*iyg*-, Das. ᵓ*ik*- (< ᵓ*ig*-), Elmolo ᵓ*ik*-; Konso *uk*-, Gidole
*k*-; HEC *ag*-; Dullay ᶜ*uk*-; Yaaku ε*k*- (< *\*ᶜag*-).[10]

*d'eg*-/*\*d'og*- (previously a prefix verb *\*-d'eg-*/-d'og-) 'hear': Saho -*edeg*- 'know, recog-
ize', Afar *dag* 'auricular region'; Somali *deg* 'ear', Rend. *dog* 'ear', *dag*- 'hear', Boni
*d'eg* 'ear' (phonemically /d'ek/), Elmolo -*tεkai*- 'hear' (probably misheard for *d'ekay*-);
;alla *d'ag-ay*- 'hear', Konso and Gidole *d'ak-ay*- 'hear'; Burji *d'ag-a* 'ear', *d'ag-ay*- 'hear';
aaku *dek*- 'hear'.

*ᵓerg*- 'send': Som. *erg-o* 'mission', Rend. *erg*-, Boni *erk*-, Das. ᵓ*erg*-; Galla *erg*-, Konso
*rk*-, Gid. *erk-iyy*- (caus.) 'lend'; Had. *erg*- 'lend', *erg-iss*- (caus.) 'borrow'; Burji
*rg*-; Gawwada *erak*-, Harso *erek*-; Yaaku *erek*-.

here is a small number of widespread cognates which offer problems in that they undoubt-
dly go back to PEC forms containing *\*g*, but show irregularities mainly caused by assimila-
:ory tendencies in the various languages. One such problem is found in the reflexes of
PEC *\*mag*ᶜ- 'name', which is firmly established on the basis of Saho-Afar *miga*ᶜ, Somali
*aga*ᶜ, Rendille *magah*, Baiso *meege*. However, Konso has *maxxa*, Gidole *mahh(a)*. Whereas
emination of the preceding consonant as a reflex of *\*ᶜ* seems regular in Konso and Gidole,
: and *h* are regular reflexes of *\*k* rather than of *\*g*. *k* is also found in Arbore *meke*ᵓ*e*.
Boni *ma*ᵓ*ag* (phonemically /ma*ᵓ*ak/) and Galla *mak'aa* fail to contribute any further evidence,
ince Boni /k/ is ambiguous, and in Galla the velar was fused with the following pharyngeal
:o yield *k'*. In Dullay, on the other hand, forms such as Gawwada *makh-akko*, Harso *makah-ko*
how the regular *k* reflex of *\*g*, but an irregular *h* reflex of *\*ᶜ*. This could be taken to
esult from assimilation to some suffix beginning in a voiceless obstruent, and may serve
as a starting point to explain the Konso and Gidole forms as resulting from double assimilation: *\*mag*ᶜ- → *\*magh* → *\*makh* → regularly *maxx*-/*mahh*-. Such an assumption would
ardly explain, however, the Arbore *k* reflex.

---

[9]In a handful of cases, the voiced allophone of /k/ has been generalized and is now
assigned to a new phoneme /g/; cf. fn. 1.

[10]There are some problematic correspondences with initial *d'*: Galla, Burji *d'ug*- 'drink',
Rendille *dug*- 'suck'. It is probable that these are reflexes of a middle voice (reflexive)
form of this same verb, *\*-t-ᶜug*- or the like.

Another dubious case is *d'agħ- 'stone', where the whole cluster is represented as zero in Saho-Afar ḍaa. Galla has d'agaa and d'akaa, which cooccur even within single dialects (e.g. in Borana). The latter shows assimilation of g to the following voiceless pharyngea while the former does not. Burji d'aha is likewise unexplained. Konso d'ak-a and Gidole d'ak-aa (Black) are regular for the k reflex of *g, but irregular as to the behavior of the cluster which should yield a geminate (cf. 4.17). A northern Gidole dialect has d'akh-a.

## 4.7.  PALATALIZATION OF *g

*g before *e and *i is palatalized to j in Somali, Galla, Rendille, and Burji, and occurs as š (from *j via *ž, and subsequently subject to general devoicing of obstruents) in Boni. One of the most obvious examples is

*gilb- 'knee': Somali jilib, Galla jilb-a, Burji jilb-a (but gilb-a is also attested), Rendille jilib, Boni šilub (pl. šilib-taa), as against Konso kilp-a, Gidole kilp(-a), Dullay kilp-ay-o, Baiso gilib; cf. also the variant *gulb- in Saho-Afar gulub, HEC *gulub- (Sidamo gulupp'-o, Hadiyya gurubb-o etc.), and probably Yaaku loi-puruk-uçi.

Cf. also Galla jidd-uu 'middle' < *gidd- (Sidamo gidd-o, Dullay kitt-e etc.),[11] Somali jir- Rendille jir-, Boni šir-, Galla jir- 'live, exist' < *gir- (Konso kir-a 'life', Baiso gir- 'exist'), Galla jald-eesa 'baboon' < *gelz- (Konso and Gidole kelt-ayta, Sidamo galad-o, Harso kals-akko etc.).

The correspondence Som. j - Rend. j - Boni š - Galla j - Burji j can thus be taken to reflect PEC *g even in cases where there is no corresponding form with g, as in Som. jeᶜel Boni še°el 'love', Galla jaal-ad'/t- 'to love' which can be reconstructed as PEC *geᶜl-.

## 4.8.  PEC *ɸ

With the exception of Yaaku all EC languages possess a voiceless labiodental (occasionally also bilabial) fricative which can be assumed to derive from a proto-phoneme PEC *ɸ. In Gidole ɸ became h mainly, but not regularly, adjacent to back vowels. In Galla, morphophonemic ɸ appears as b before s and l and as m before nasals.

The regular Yaaku reflex of *ɸ is p. There is some evidence that PEC *ɸ goes further back to Proto-Cushitic *p (cf. Dolgopol'skiy (1973)); there are in fact some alternations between PEC *ɸ and PEC *b which are perhaps amenable to explanation as resulting from assimilation of voice at an early date where *ɸ was still *p. At present, however, there is nothing to suggest the necessity of reconstructing PEC *p. The mass of evidence (24 languages with ɸ and only one with p) is taken here as a guarantee for PEC *ɸ; it is assumed that PEC *ɸ became p in Yaaku.

In a few words *ɸɸ has been reconstructed; this yields ɸɸ in Konso-Gidole, HEC, Burji and Dullay, ɸ(ɸ) in Dasenech, and ɸ in Somali, Rendille and Boni. Nothing is known on the reflexes of geminate *ɸɸ in other languages.

Examples of initial *ɸ:

*ɸal- 'to curse': Somali ɸal- 'bewitch', Rendille ɸal- 'curse', Dasenech ɸal-m- 'lie'; Galla ɸal-ɸal-a 'cattivo soggetto'; hadiyya ɸar- 'bewitch'.

---

[11]Perhaps the Somali tribal name Jidd-u is also related, if it may be interpreted as 'those who are in the center', just as Midgaan is 'those who are to the right (midig).

*ɓil- 'to comb': Saho ɓiil-, Afar ɓil-; Rendille ɓil-, Boni ɓil-; Galla ɓil-, Konso ɓil-; Sidamo ɓil-; Burji ɓil-; Dullay ɓill-.  Somali ɓeed'- 'id.' is probably cognate.

*ɓur- 'open, free, untie': Somali ɓur-, Rendille ɓur-, Boni ɓur-, Das. ɓur-; Galla ɓur-, Konso ɓur-, Gidole ɓur-iyy- (Black), hur- (Sasse); Burji ɓur-. Hadiyya hor- 'id.' is probably cognate, but shows an otherwise unattested h reflex (cf. however Hadiyya tuɓ- ~ tuh- 'spit').

Examples of medial *ɓ:

*ʾaɓ- 'mouth': Saho-Afar aɓ; Somali aɓ, Rendille aɓ, Boni aɓ, Dasenech ʾaɓ-u; Galla aɓ-aani (pl.), Konso aɓ-aa (pl.); Sidamo, Darasa, Alaba aɓ-o, Hadiyya aɓ-o(ʾ)o 'hole'; Burji aɓ-a.

*riɓ- 'pluck': Som. riɓ- 'pluck (poultry)', pass. 'be frayed', Das. riɓ- 'pull out (hair or feather)'; Galla riɓ- 'pluck, flay, pull out hair', Gidole riɓ- 'pull out a hair'; Burji riɓ- 'pluck'. A derivation from this verb is a common word for 'hair', PEC *riɓ-an-: Elmolo rupan, Arbore riyɓan; Galla riɓeen-sa (< *riɓan-ita), Konso nyirɓ-a (by metathesis), Gidole riɓan-t (Northern Gidole riɓan-ta 'fur'); Harso riɓan-ko 'body-hair'.

*k'uɓ(a)ᶜ- 'cough': Saho uɓuᶜ-; Boni uɓaʾ-, Somali quɓaᶜ-, Elmolo yu·ɓ, Dasenech g'uɓ-; Galla k'uɓa-; Burji k'uɓ-ey-; Harso guɓaᶜ-; Yaaku qopɛʾɛ-.

Examples of *ɓɓ include:

*ʾuɓɓ- 'blow': Saho uɓ-u- 'breathe', Afar uɓɓ-uy 'breath'; Das., ʾuɓ- 'blow'; Galla uɓɓi jed'- 'blow', Konso uɓɓ- 'inflate', Gidole uɓɓ- 'blow'; Hadiyya uɓɓ- 'blow (fire)'; Dullay uɓɓ- 'blow, inflate'. Sidamo and Burji uɓuɓ- are cognate, but reflect a different base.

## 4.9.  PEC *z

The existence of a PEC voiced sibilant *z has only recently been rediscovered, although Cerulli had already reconstructed it on the basis of a very small amount of evidence.[12] In Sasse (1976a) I published a considerable amount of data and arguments in support of *z mainly on the basis of the limited material available at that time.  Since then, a vast body of data from languages highly indicative of PEC *z became available to me through the collection of Dullay material by Amborn and Minker and the study of Rendille by Heine (1976).  In his recent comparative study of Somali, Boni, and Rendille (1978b), Heine was able to reconstruct more than a dozen roots containing *z, most of which are congruent with PEC *z roots arrived at by the comparison of other languages.  Since it would be tedious to repeat all the considerations already presented in Sasse (1976a), I will take the existence of PEC *z for granted and propose some of the new etymologies that became possible with the help of the new material mentioned above.

The reflexes of PEC *z are as follows:  Saho-Afar d (in one case t through assimilation), except for some northern Saho dialects where z (in alternation with ð), still survives, Somali northern dialects d, southern dialects y, Rendille y, Boni d, Arbore z, Dasenech z (in alternation with ð), Elmolo y and w in the environment of back and front vowels, respectively, Galla d, Konso and Gidole t (s in a handful of cases, see below), HEC d except Alaba z, Burji d, Dullay s, Yaaku z.

Examples of initial *z:

---

[12]Black was not able to reconstruct PEC *z because most of the languages he deals with do not distinguish between reflexes of *d and *z.

*zagm- 'honey': Galla damm-a, Konso takm-a, Gidole tank-(a) (by metathesis); Gawwada, Harso, and Gollango sakm-o; Yaaku sika', pl. sakm-ai.

*zit- 'pull': Konso tit-, Gidole tiš-; Burji did- (by assimilation); Gawwada, Gollango sit- Harso sic-. Somali jiid-, Rendille jit-, and Boni šid- are perhaps cognate, although they display the normal reflexes of palatalized *g (perhaps via *ž, i.e. palatalization of *z before i?).

What was originally a prefix verb in PEC *-zrig-/*-zrug-, and still survives in Saho -izrig-, -idrig- 'stir', became suffixing in Somali durk-/durug 'shift one's position', Elmolo yuruk- 'push', and Arbore zarug- 'push'. Gidole tukkur- 'push', Konso tuqquur- 'shove', and Dullay sukkur- 'push, shove' are obviously cognate.[13]

Examples of medial *z:

*baz- 'lake, sea': Saho-Afar bad 'sea'; Somali bad 'sea', Rendille bey 'lake', Dasenech baz 'Lake Rudolf', Elmolo paw 'Lake Rudolf'; Gollango and Dobase pas-o 'lake'.

*wazn- 'heart': Saho wazana, wadana; Somali wadne, Rendille weyn-a, Boni wenn-e', wend-ᵉ, Dasenech wozin-ni; Galla onn-ee, Konso otan-ta 'center'; Sidamo wadan-a, Kambata wazan-a, Alaba wozan-a.

*gelz- 'baboon': Galla jald-eesa , Konso and Gidole kelt-ayta; Sidamo galad-o; Burji geld-ey; Dullay kals-akko.

An example of *zz is

*ḥizz- 'root': Somali ḥidid, Rendille ḥiy, pl. ḥiy-ay, Boni hiid-ᵉ, pl. hiitt-ᵉ', Arbore hiyds-o (probably pl. /hizz-o/), Dasenech hiz, pl. hizz-u; Elmolo hiw-ε'; Galla hidd-a, Konso hitt-ina, Gidole hitt-in(a); Gawwada ḥiss-e, Harso ḥiis-e.

4.10.  PEC *x?

There are two languages, Dullay and Yaaku, whose phoneme inventories include a voiceless velar (occasionally also uvular) fricative x apparently non-derivable from any hitherto established proto-phoneme. In Harso, /x/ is in contrast with /h/ which regularly derives from *k. In most other Dullay dialects x does not appear to be phonemically distinct from /h/, but can be geminated as xx, whereas geminated *kk yields only kk, never xx or hh, cf. paxx-e, pl. of pax-te 'hair' vs. lakki 'two' from *lakk-. In Yaaku, the regular reflex of *k is k, except when palatalized to ç. However, the phoneme x occurs in all environments in a considerable number of words.

Interestingly enough, there are at least three clear correspondences between Harso x and Yaaku x:

    Harso xupin, Yaaku xoopi 'five'
    Harso lax-ko, 'arrow poison', Yaaku lax 'arrow'
    Harso ax-icce, pl. axx-e 'eye', Yaaku wax- 'see'

To these may eventually be added Harso xuc'-, Yaaku çaq- 'be full', as Yaaku x appears to alternate with ç.

---

[13]Gawwada (Black) has suqqur- with the same irregular q reflex of *g as in Konso. It is obvious that borrowing or at least mutual adjustment of forms due to language contact is at work here, since the majority of the Gawwada community is reported as being bilingual in Konso and Gawwada.

The remainder of the EC languages present some possible cognates to these words; the correspondences of *x* do not, however, appear to be unifiable. A *w* reflex is shown in Galla *law-aa*, Konso *law-itta*, *law-a* 'arrow'. All forms could probably be subsumed under a reconstruction *\*lawx-*, if a zero reflex of *x* in Macro-Oromo is assumed. A zero reflex of *x* is also shown in Yaaku *naxap*, Galla and Burji *naɓ-a* 'body' (*\*naxɓ-*?). On the other hand, *ax-/wax-* appear to be cognate to Galla *akeek-* 'observe, examine, regard' and Konso-Gidole *akk-* 'see'. Harso *poox-* 'swell', Hadiyya *bokk-* 'rise (of dough)', Somali *boog* 'ulcer'. Cf. also Konso *oxin-ta* 'fence' with unexplained *x* (in Konso *x* does not normally occur before *i*) = Yaaku *waxn-o'* 'id.'.

It is possible that further studies will reveal the necessity of reconstructing a proto-phoneme *\*x*. In the meantime, it seems preferable to attribute the development of *x* to a common innovation of Yaaku and Dullay. This would not be the only one; despite their geographical distance Yaaku and the Dullay dialects share some interesting lexical and morphological peculiarities.

## 4.11.   PEC *\*l*

The liquid *\*l* continues as *l* in all EC languages except Hadiyya, where it split into *r* and *l*, the former occurring intervocalically, the latter elsewhere.

On some individual deviations see below.

Examples of initial *\*l*:

*\*lam(m)-* 'two': Saho *lamm-a*, Afar *lamm-ay*; Somali Isaaq *lab-a* (cf. 4.14), southern *lamm-a*, Rendille *lam-a*, Boni *low'*, Arbore *lam-a-*, Elmolo /laam-a/ (pronounced [ra:ma'], cf. Heine (1977)); Baiso *lam(m)-a*; Galla *lam-a*, Konso *lam-itta* 'son of second wife', *lam-atti* 'both of you', *lamm-aaw-* 'become two, happen twice'; Sidamo *lam(m)-e*, Hadiyya *lam-o*; Burji *lam-a*; Dobase *lamm-ay*. Dasenech *naam-a* shows assimilation of *l* to *m*.

*\*luk'm-* 'neck': Somali *luqun*, pl. *luqum-o*, Rendille *luxum*, Boni *nuᵊun'* (with assimilation of *l* to *n*), Arbore *luko* (or *luk-o*?), Dasenech *luu-tti*, Elmolo *luk*, pl. *luum-ʊ'*; Galla *lumm-ee* 'neck of ox'; Hadiyya *loom-e* 'Adam's apple'.

*\*laɓ-* 'bone': Saho-Afar *laɓ-a*; Somali *laɓ*, Rendille *laɓ*, Boni *laɓ*, Arbore *leɓ*, Dasenech *laɓ-itti*, Elmolo /laf-a/ (pronounced [rafa'], cf. Heine (1977)), Baiso *leɓ-i*; Galla *laɓ-ee*, Konso *laɓ-ta*, Gidole *laɓ-t(a)*.

Examples of medial *\*l*:

*\*ᶜol-* 'war': Somali *ᶜol* 'enemy', Rendille *hol*, Boni *ol*, Elmolo *is-olol-* 'quarrel'; Galla *lool-* 'fight' (< *olool-* < *\*ᶜolᶜol-*); Hadiyya *or-a*.

*\*d'al-* 'beget, give birth': Saho-Afar *dal-*; Somali *dal-*, Rendille *del-*, Boni *d'el-̩*, Dasenech *d'al-*; Galla *d'al-*, Konso *d'al-/d'el-*, Gidole *d'al-*; Burji *d'al-*; Dullay *d'al-*; Yaaku *del-*.

*\*malh-* 'pus': Saho-Afar *malah*; Somali *malah*, Dasenech *mel-tti*; Galla *mala-a*, Konso *mal-a*, Gidole *malh-(a)*, *mall-(a)*; Sidamo *mal-a*, Hadiyya *mar-a*; Burji *mal-a*; Gawwada *malh-akko*, Harso and Gollango *malah-ko*; Yaaku *milɛh*.

There are three known cases of palatalization of *\*l* into *j* in Galla:

*jah-a* 'moon' < PEC *\*leᶜ-* as in Konso *le-a*, Gidole *leh-a*; Dullay *leᶜ-o*; Yaaku *lɛɛᵊ*; Arbore *leh*, Elmolo *lɛ·ᵊ*.

*jah-a, jaa* 'six' < PEC *liħ-* as in Saho *liħ*, Afar *leħ-ey*; Somali and Rendille *liħ*, Boni *liħ*, Dasenech *li* etc.  The Galla form actually derives from a variant *leħ* which is also found in Baiso *leh*, Konso *leh*, Gidole *leh(-e)* etc.

dial. *ij-a, ijj-a* 'eye' (Borana *il-a*) < PEC *ʔil-* as in Somali, Boni, Rendille *il*, Dasenec *ʔil*, Elmolo *il*, Baiso *il-i*; Konso *il-ta*, Gidole *il-t(a)*; HEC *ill-*; Burji *il-a*; Yaaku *il*. It is not likely that the preceding *i* is responsible for the palatalization here; *ij(j)-a* probably derives from earlier *ij-sa < *il-ita*.

Perhaps also Galla *jab-* 'strong' contains a former *l*.  It may be related to PEC *lab-* 'big, male' which is reflected in Saho-Afar *lab*, Som. *lab*, Sidamo *lab-a* 'male', *lab-o* 'big many' etc.

Several cases of irregular palatalizations of *l* into *y* have been observed in Dasenech and Elmolo.  The Dasenech reflex of *lab-* 'male' is *yab* (perhaps *yeb*; *a* and *e* are not distinc after *y*), which together with the evidence of Elmolo *lep* 'id.' points to a reconstruction *leb-* rather than *lab-*.  This would even better motivate Galla *jab-aa* cited above. Elmolo has a *y* reflex in *yiiʔ* 'six' < PEC *liħ-*.

An occasional shift of *l* to *n* occurred in some languages as a result of assimilation in the neighborhood of nasals, cf. Dasenech *naam-a* 'two' and Boni *nuʔun'* 'neck' cited above.

There is also some fluctuation between *l* and *r*, especially in the environment of glottals and glottalized stops, e.g. PEC *k'olɓ-* 'bark' becomes Saho *koroɓ-o*, *ʔilk-* 'tooth' becomes Burji *irk'-a*, *leʔ-* 'die' Sidamo and Kambata *reʔ-* etc.

As a member of consonant clusters, *l* is usually stable.  In Galla *l + n* and *n + l* both become *ll*; similar contractions are observed in many other EC languages.  There is some evidence that *l* is deleted in the environment *i___C* in Saho-Afar, cf. *ʔilk-* 'tooth' → *ik-o*, *d'₁ilħ=* → *dilħ-eno ~ diħ-eno* 'charcoal'.

As far as can be gathered from scattered indications, PEC *ll* continues as *ll* in all EC languages.  I was unable, however, to reconstruct any widespread PEC root containing root-internal *ll*.  The cognate set comprising Saho *all-o* 'vanity, nothingness', Galla *k'all-aa* 'subtle, thin, meagre', Konso *qallaʔ-* 'thin', Gidole *k'allaʔ-* 'narrow', Burji *k'all-anee-* 'thin' may perhaps be a case in point (PEC *k'all-* 'thin, insignificant'), but the Borana equivalent *k'ald'-a'* also suggests a reconstruction *k'alʔ-*, in which case the Konso and Gidole forms may be taken to represent a former distributive formation with its typical gemination, just as PEC *bald'-* 'broad' yields Somali *ballaad.*

## 4.12.  PEC *r

PEC *r* survives as such in all EC languages except Hadiyya, where it merged with *l* to yield *r* intervocalically, *l* elsewhere.

Examples of initial *r*:

*raɓ-* 'sleep': Dasenech *raɓ-* 'spend the night', Elmolo *rap-*; Galla *raɓ-*; Hadiyya *lap'-*; Gawwada *raɓ-*, Harso, Dobase, and Gollango *raɓ-* 'spend the night'.

*riʔ-* 'goat': Somali *ri(ʔ)*, Rendille *riħ-i*; Galla *reʔ-ee*; Yaaku *rɛh-ɛ'* 'calf'.

*roob-* 'rain': Saho-Afar *rob*; Somali *roob*, Rendille *roob* 'green country', Boni *roob*; Galla *roob-a*, Konso *roop-a*, Gidole *roop(-a)*.

Examples of medial *r*:

*mur- 'cut, judge': Dasenech mur-, Elmolo and Arbore mur-i- 'short'; Galla mur-, Gidole
mur- 'cut person's genitals to take trophy', Konso mur-; HEC (Sid., Had.) mur-; Burji
mur-. Perhaps Dullay murr- 'pay' is also cognate.

*door- 'choose': Saho door-, Afar dor-; Somali door-; Sidamo dor-; Yaaku door-ta-.

*ʔorg- (original meaning difficult to determine): Somali org-i 'billy-goat'; Galla org-ee
'baby she-camel', Gidole ork-eta 'billy-goat' (Black: ork-eet 'non-castrated male goat
older than ca. two months'); Harso ork-akko 'billy-goat'; Yaaku org-ei 'male giraffe'.
Cf. also Somali agor 'bull-calf to two years old', Rendille ogor 'gazelle'.

The occurrence of *r in consonant clusters does not normally affect its reflexes in the
individual languages. It assimilates preceding or following n in Galla and some other
languages, but apparently not in Saho-Afar, Konso-Gidole; in Somali this process is
optional. An example of the cluster *rn is *sirn-/*surn- 'nasal mucus' which continues
as Saho sinr-aaᶜ/sunr-aaᶜ (Reinisch; by metathesis and with unexplained extensions),
Galla furr-ii, Konso sorn-eeta, and Harso surun-ho.

In Dasenech the cluster *rt (also *rd and *rd') shows the unusual reflex dd'. In addition
to morphophonemic evidence, there is only one PEC root containing *rd which shows this
reflex: *-rd- 'run' yields Dasenech ;ʔadd'-um- 'dance, play'.

An example of PEC *rr is probably

;ʔarrab- 'tongue', with a by-form *ᶜarrab- forming the basis of at least the Omo-Tana
and Yaaku cognates (the Macro-Oromo, HEC, and Burji forms are inconclusive): Afar arrab-a;
Somali ᶜarrab, Rendille harrab, Boni arub, Dasenech, ʔere, Elmolo ʔerrep , Baiso irreb-i;
Galla arrab-a, Konso arrap-a, Gidole arrap(-a); Sidamo and Darasa arrab-a, Hadiyya
allaab-o; Burji arrab-a; Dullay arrap-ko; Yaaku ere, pl. erep-a. The geminate rr in this
root may possibly result from a very old assimilation of the cluster *nr, cf. the Saho
cognate anrab.

## 4.13. PEC *n

The denti-alveolar nasal *n appears to survive as such in all EC languages. It became
assimilated to adjacent r and l as stated in 4.11 and 4.12, and was palatalized into ny
regularly before and after i in Dasenech. n after y yields ny in Northern Galla, nn
in Borana; *ne yields Galla nya. Final n often becomes n in some southern Somali and
Boni dialects.

Examples of initial *n:

*nah- 'fear': Somali nah- 'pity, be startled'; Galla nah- 'fear, take pity on', Konso
nah- 'be tender hearted', Gidole nah- 'be afraid, tremble'; Burji na- 'fear'.

*nass-/*ness- 'breathe, rest': Somali nas-ad-, Rendille nas-, Elmolo nas-i; Galla naf-ii
'energy'(?), Konso ness-a 'soul, breath, noise', Gidole nass 'voice, character'; Dullay
nass-ad'- 'breathe', nass-o 'soul, life, spirit, breath'; Yaaku nes-i 'breath' (only in
compounds).

*neᶜb- (originally a verb of the prefix conjugation *-nᶜeb-) 'hate': Saho-Afar -nᶜeb-
(pref.) 'hate', naᶜab-toli 'enemy'; Somali neᶜeb 'hatred', Dasenech neb 'dislike', neeb-eze
'hate'; Galla nyaap'-a 'enemy'; Burji nab-i 'enemy'.

Examples of medial *n:

*man-/*min- 'house': Somali Isaaq (arch.) min 'bridal house', southern min 'room', min-an (pl.) 'house', Rendille min, Boni miŋ, pl. min-t$^{eʔ}$, Elmolo min; Galla man-a, Konso man-a, Gidole man-a; Sidamo, Darasa, Hadiyya min-e, Alaba min-o; Burji min-a; Dullay man-o.

*ʔinam-/*ʔinm- m. 'son, boy', f. 'daughter, girl': Somali inan, pl. inamm-o 'boy, son', inán, pl. inam-o 'girl, daughter', Rendille inam 'boy', inām 'girl, daughter'; Konso inn-a 'son, boy', inan-ta 'girl, daughter', Gidole imm(-a) 'son, boy', inan-t(a) 'girl, daughter'; Harso inan-ko 'son-in-law'.

*ħand'ur-/*ħund'ur- 'navel': Somali ħuɖur, Rendille hanɖur, Boni hanuur', Elmolo ʊnyur'; Galla hand'uur-a, Gidole hund'uur-t (Sasse huɲʔur-ta); Burji hanʔur-a; Gawwada hund'ur-te, Harso ħand'ur-ce ~ ħund'ur-cẹ; Yaaku hender-o, pl. hendor-mai. Dasenech ʔonyir is cognate, but shows irregular loss of *ħ (normally → h).

This last example demonstrates the behavior of the cluster *nd', which yields nʔ in some Macro-Oromo varieties and in Burji, ny in Elmolo, n in Boni and nn in Dasenech (in the Dasenech example this was later palatalized to ny, but cf. Das. sinn-a 'urine' from PEC *sind'$_1$-.

There is a strong tendency for *n to become l, either as a result of dissimilation, if the root contains some other nasal consonant, or apparently unmotivated. Numerous cases have been observed in various languages, e.g. PEC *nam- (also *nim-/*num- 'man', Saho-Afar num, Somali nin, pl. nim-an, Galla, Konso, Gidole nam-a) became lamm-a in Burji; PEC *nuug- 'suck' (Som., Boni nuug-, Rend. nug-, Elmolo, Yaaku nuuk-) became Macro-Oromo *luug- (Galla luug-, Konso luuk-); PEC *nab- 'smear' (Somali nab- 'stick', Konso nap- 'paint with soot') became Hadiyya lapp- 'paint, anoint'; PEC *nabħ- 'ear' (Rendille nabaħ, Konso napah-ata etc.) became Gidole lap-itt(a), and many others.

No sufficiently wide-spread root with *nn has been reconstructed, but cf. *kann-/*kinn- 'bee', Somali sinn-i, Galla kann-i-sa (Borana kinn-ii-sa < kann-ii-sa); however, Konso and Gidole have xan-ta and han-t(a) respectively with single n.


## 4.14.  PEC *m

PEC *m is represented as such in all EC languages. The only major special development is found in Eastern Omo-Tana (Somali, Boni, Rendille) which is characterized by a morpho-phonemic rule m → n/ ___#. This rule is still alive in Somali and Boni, but was given up in Rendille, leaving several instances of false analogy (e.g. PEC *san- 'nose' became Rendille sam). Gioloe and Dullay have a morphophonemic rule of nasal assimilation (points-of-articulation features of nasals are assimilated to a following obstruent; hence m occurs as n before dentals and as ŋ before back consonants. In some languages m → n before n. In Dasenech the cluster mt yields nn; hence stem-final /m/ was often generalized as n (e.g. tun- < PEC *tum-).

Examples of initial *m:

*mar- 'round; vb. roll (up)': Afar mar-o 'round', Aussa dialect mar-to 'skirt'; Somali mar 'waïst', mar- 'pass', mar-s-t- (caus. refl.) 'put on clothes (woman)', mar-o 'cloth', Rend. mar- 'be round', Boni mar- 'be round', mar-i' 'clothes', Das. maad'- 'turn around' (d' through analogy to the second person maadd'a where dd' is regularly < *rt), Elmolo warai-mara 'round', Baiso mar-amure 'round'; Galla mar- 'roll up', mar-s- (fossilized caus.) 'encompass, encircle', Konso mar- 'roll up' (e.g. cloth, thread), mar-š- (fossilized caus.) 'go in a group to attack someone', Gidole mar- 'coil rope, rool cloth'; HEC mar- 'go'; Gollango and Dobase mar- 'coil'. Somali marmar 'nape of neck', Burji marmar(-i) 'nec and Galla morm-a 'neck' also belong to this root. Cf. also Somali meer- 'roam' and meer-sa 'round'.

*mig-/*mug- 'full(ness)', derived from a former prefix verb *-mg- 'fill': Saho mig-e 'fullness', -meg- (pref.) 'fill', Afar -eng- (< *-emg-)'fill'; Somali mug 'fullness', Baiso
mig-i 'full'; Galla mog-a 'fullness', mij-uu 'full'; Yaaku mok 'many'. Konso immak-,
Gidole innak- 'fill' are obviously cognate, but display problematic correspondences.

*mizg- 'right-hand (side)': Saho midg-a, (dial.) mizg-a, Afar midg-a, (dial.) migid-a (by
metathesis); Somali midig, Jiddu meyg-, Rendille miig (< *miyig), Boni midig; Galla mirg-a,
Konso mikt-a (by metathesis), Gidole misk-itt; Dullay misik-ko. Arbore and Burji mirg-a are
loans from Galla.  Hadiyya makk-a is possibly cognate, but displays problematic correspondences.

Examples of medial *m:

*k'om- 'chew, bite, eat', derived from a former prefix verb *-k'(o)m-: Saho -qom- (pref.),
Afar -okm- (pref.); Somali qoon 'wound', qoom- 'to wound', Das. kom! (imper.) 'eat!' (k is
due to the former clustering of k' and m, cf. *-k'sol- 'laugh' → kosol-); Galla k'am-
'chew č'at', Konso qom- '(1) chew; (2) ache'; Hadiyya om-ara 'wound'. Gollango qan- 'chew'
may be related, if n is taken to result from analogy, but may otherwise be cognate with
PEC *k'aniin- 'bite'.

*kum- 'thousand': Somali kun, pl. kum-an; Galla kum-a, Konso kum-a; Sidamo kum-e, Hadiyya
kum-a; Burji kum-a.  Gollango and Harso kum-a must be loans from Galla or Konso, because
otherwise *kuma would be expected.

*d'amh- 'cold': Saho ḍamaḥ; Somali ḍaḥan 'cold', ḍaḥam-ood- 'become cold', Boni d'ahan,
Dasenech d'eeny (< *d'ahan); Galla d'aam-od'/t- (< *d'aḥm-ood'/t-) 'feel cold', Konso
d'am-aad'- 'become cold', Gidole d'amh-ad'-, d'amm-ad'- 'become cold'; Yaaku dɛhm-o 'cold'.

An example of *mm is

*ʔamm(-an)- 'time, now': Somali amm-in-ka, imm-in-ka, imm-i-ka 'now'; Galla amm-a 'now',
Konso amm-a 'now', Gidole amm-an-n-e; Hadiyya amm-an-i 'time, when'.

In a handful of instances intervocalic *m becomes b in Somali: *lam- 'two': Som. laba;
*toman 'ten': Som. toban; Boni kamis, Southern Somali kimis 'bread': Northern Som. kibis;
Boni duumaal- 'swim': Som. dabaal-. Heine (1978b)         tentatively posits the cluster
*mm to account for this correspondence.  This may be a possible explanation, but is not
without difficulties, because the cluster mm is actually existent in Somali, and in at
least one instance (*ʔamm-an- 'now') it appears to reflect PEC *mm.  Moreover, a b reflex
of intervocalic *m is also shown in Afar toban 'ten'.  At the present state of our knowledge, no plausible solution to this problem is apparent.


4.15.   PEC *d' AND d'₁ OR EVEN MORE *d' 's?

The reconstruction of PEC glottalized (or otherwise affected) stops in the denti-alveolar
region seems unproblematic as long as the principal "Lowland East Cushitic" languages are
examined, but becomes more and more complicated once other languages are taken into con-
sideration.  Saho-Afar, Somali, Boni, Rendille, Dasenech, and possibly also Arbore and
Elmolo have only one such sound in their phonemic inventories, which is normally symbolized
as ḍ (a voiced retroflex stop) in Saho-Afar, Somali, and Rendille, and as d' in Boni and
Dasenech.  The symbol d' seems appropriate also for Arbore and Elmolo; it denotes slightly
different varieties of a (pre)glottalized and implosive d.  These phonemes regularly correspond to each other, as can be seen from the following examples:

Afar ḍis-; Somali ḍis-, Rendille ḍis-, Boni d'is-, Dasenech d'is- 'plant, build'.

Saho ɖamaħ; Somali ɖahan, Boni d'ahan, Dasenech d'eeny 'cold'.

This phoneme regularly corresponds to Macro-Oromo d' and may in fact be reconstructed as "Proto-Lowland-East-Cushitic" *d':

*d'iš- 'plant, build': Galla d'iš- 'stretch out skin', Konso d'iš- 'plant'.

*d'amħ- 'cold': cf. 4.14.

Things then become complicated since d' is not the only glottalized stop of the coronal series in Galla, Konso, and Gidole. Galla and Gidole have also t' and c', and Konso has also ʄ, a palatal implosive. In a good many cases Galla c' is a palatalized reflex of *k', as already stated in 3.6 above. In other instances, however, c' corresponds to d' in the other languages:

c'ik'il-ee 'elbow': Konso d'ikl-a, Gidole d'ilk.

c'il-ee 'charcoal': Somali duħul, Konso d'il-a, Gidole d'ilh-a.

c'uɓ- 'close': Gidole d'uh-, Konso d'uɓ- 'close'.

ɓinc'-aani 'urine': Konso, Gidole sind'-aa, Arbore sind'- 'urinate'.

hanc'uɓ-a 'spittle': Somali ʕanɖuuɓ.

miic'- 'wash clothes': Som. mayɖ-.

It is impossible to account for these c' reflexes in terms of an environmentally conditione phonemic split, e.g. *d' → c' before front vowels and u (and analogically generalized in miic'- and ɓinc'-aani), since numerous instances of well-supported reconstructions of PEC *d' before front vowels and u, which all yield Galla reflexes with d', would immediately invalidate such an hypothesis (cf. *d'iš- quoted above, also *d'iit- 'kick', → d'iit-, *d'ibb- 'hundred' → d'ibb-a, *d'ug- 'truth' → d'ug-aa, *d'ung- 'kiss' → d'ung-, *d'uus- 'fart' → d'uuɓ- etc.). A second and more plausible possibility would be to assume a second proto-phoneme, say *d'$_1$, which could be assumed to merge with *d' in Somali, Rendille etc. but to yield distinct reflexes in Galla at least in certain enviornments.

Galla t' mainly occurs either in loanwords or in roots of a descriptive nature. It might thus be considered secondary, were it not for the fact that there are at least three words with t' which have such widespread and formally different cognates in other languages that borrowing would be a poor explanation. The first one, which also demonstrates the argument of autochthony on the basis of formal difference, is ɓalat'-a 'log' (also vb. ɓalat'- 'cut wood' and other derivations) which is cognate with Somali ɓalliiɖ 'a chip of wood', and Saho -ɓliɖ- 'split'. There exists an Ethiosemitic root ɓ-l-ṣ or ɓ-l-ṭ with a similar meaning, but it is unlikely that the Somali and Saho words have been borrowed from this root, because Somali and Saho ɖ is not the regular way to integrate Ethiosemitic ṣ or ṭ. There is, moreover, a Yaaku cognate which cannot possibly have been borrowed from Semitic. (Cf. p. 31 below.) The other two apparently autochthonous t' words of Galla, k'urt'umm-ii 'fish' and t'ur- 'be dirty' will be considered below.

There is nothing to suggest that Gidole t' is anything more than a loan phoneme. Nearly 90% of its occurrence are restricted to recent borrowings from Amharic or some Omotic language, and the rest may also be loans whose source happens to be unknown to me. At any event, I have found no instance of Gidole t' that would necessitate an autochthonous interpretation.

This is not the case with Gidole c' and Konso ʄ. These two phonemes are in regular correspondence with each other, as the following cognate sets clearly demonstrate:

G  c'aacc'-  'discuss'           =  K  jaajj-  'make noise'

G  c'aal-    'be better, wealth-  =  K  jaal-   'exceed, be bigger, longer'
                ier, taller'

G  c'ik'-    'wash'               =  K  jaq-    'wash'

G  c'iɓ-     'grow tall, stretch  =  K  jiɓ-    'grow tall'
                oneself'

G  c'irɓ-    'braid'              =  K  jirɓ-   'braid'

G  c'ool-    'become blind'       =  K  jool-   'be blind'

G  ɓuuc'-    'drizzle'            =  K  ɓuuj-   'whistle'
(because of the hissing sound produced by a drizzle)

G  hinc'ir-et  'type of small     =  K  hinjirr-eta  'anything red'
                red ant'

G  koc'-     'little in amount'    =  K  qoj-    'pinch; take a small piece'

G  pooc'-    'take by force'       =  K  pooj-   'capture'

There are some more correspondences which suggest borrowing and are therefore to be discarded.  On the whole, however, both the great number of corresponding items and the nature of the words involved suggest that borrowing is not a major source of all these cognates.  Konso $j$ is otherwise the regular means by which Amharic and Galla $c'$ is integrated:  jarq-eta 'cloth' < Amh. c'ärq, jiqil- 'measure in cubits' < Bor. c'ik'il-.

In order to account for the correspondence between Konso $j$ and Gidole $c'$, it would seem appropriate to reconstruct a phoneme Proto-Konso-Gidole *$c'$ which remained as such in Gidole and became $j$ in Konso.  This is also in accordance with the overall picture of the development of the Konso sound system which shows a strong tendency towards voicing of non-plain stops ($k' \rightarrow q$ [G], $c' \rightarrow j$).

Three of the reconstructions arrived at in this way have cognates with $c'$ in Galla:

PKG  *c'aal-   'exceed'           =  Galla  c'aal-  'id.'

PKG  *c'iɓ-    'grow tall,        =  Galla  c'iiɓ-  'stretch oneself, lie down'
                stretch oneself'

PKG  *c'irɓ-   'braid'            =  Galla  c'iɓr-aa  'women's hairdo'

There are further comparisons involving the correspondence Konso $j$ = Galla $c'$ (no Gidole cognates are attested):

K  jaɓɓ-eta  'green grassy        =  Galla  c'aɓɓ-ee  'id.'
                area'

K  jeer-     'be ashamed'         =  Galla  c'eer-   'id.'

It seems consistent to assign these five correspondences to *$d'_1$:  (1) *$d'_1aal$-, (2) *$d'_1i(i)ɓ$-, (3) *$d'_1iɓr$-, (4) *$d'_1aɓɓ$-, (5) *$d'_1eer$-.  No. 4 may indeed be a loanword.

There is one case which involves the correspondence PKG *$c'$ = Galla $d'$:  PKG *$c'ak'$-/ *$c'ik'$- 'wash' = Galla $d'ik'$- 'id.'.  This correspondence is interesting in several respects.  First of all, it demonstrates that there may exist $d'$ reflexes of *$d'_1$ in Galla even before $i$, where we would expect $c'$.  An inconsistency like this can be explained in a variety of ways.  It would certainly be possible to restrict *$d'_1$ to the correspondence

Gidole  $c'$  = Konso  $j$  = Galla  $c'$

and to set up a third glottalized dental  $*d'_2$  to account for the correspondence

Gidole  $c'$  = Konso  $j$  = Galla  $d'$

Another alternative would be the assumption of a tendency in some Galla dialect(s) to merge  $*d'$  and  $*d'_1$  (on the model of other EC languages such as Somali etc.) and a subsequent diffusion through dialect or sociolect borrowing. That the second alternative is the more plausible can be seen from the fact that such inconsistencies occur even within the Konso-Gidole group itself. Strangely enough, some varieties of Gidole also use a form  $d'ik'$- 'wash', and in such a case "borrowing from Galla" is but a simplistic explanation. Moreover, there is another instance of Konso  $j$  corresponding to Gidole  $d'$, and this time borrowing is clearly out of the question:  $jiraat-i$  'Gidole' = Gidole  $d'iraaš$  'id.'. On the other hand, we find instances of Galla  $c'$  versus Konso AND Gidole  $d'$:  $finc'-aani$  'urine' and  $c'ik'il-ee$  'elbow', both already cited above. Finally there are instances of Gidole  $c'$  where both Konso and Galla display  $d'$  instead of the expected  $j$  or  $c'$, respectively:

Gidole  $mic'-a$  'edible leaves': Konso  $mid'-aa$  'id.', Galla  $mid'-aani$  'fruit, grain'.

Gidole  $c'iip$-  'squeeze': Konso  $d'iipp$-  'id.', Galla  $d'iib$-  'push, bother'.

There is even one case in which the same Gidole dialect has both variants in different words:  $c'okk'-a$  'mud',  $d'okk'-itot$  'quicksand'.

To sum up: it seems that all possible combinations of reflexes may occur, and that the original distribution of  $d'$ ,  $c'$  and  $j$  has been terribly distorted. On the other hand, the case of Galla  $d'ik'$- vs. Konso  $jaq$- and Gidole  $c'ik'$- proves unequivocally that PKG  $*c'$  cannot be a loan phoneme; it must clearly derive from a proto-phoneme distinct from PEC  $*d'$ . Galla as a possible source is out of the question, since it has neither the  $c'$  reflex in this particular word for 'wash', nor the  $a$  vocalization of the Konso form, and Dullay is even more out of the question, because it entirely lacks this root. In other words, we have to confine ourselves to the following unsatisfactory statements: all three Macro-Oromo languages present traces of a proto-phoneme  $*d'_1$ , in so far as each of them has a particular phoneme which may be regarded as a possible reflex of  $*d'_1$ , and in at least some cases cognate sets can be established which show a certain degree of regular correspondence. Upon inspection of these cognate sets a rule can be abstracted which says that  $*d'_1$  should regularly yield  $c'$  in Galla and in Gidole, and  $j$  in Konso, at least in certain as yet undetermined environments. However,  $*d'_1$  may also appear as  $d'$  in all three languages. In order to keep our reconstruction as neat as possible, we may wish to formulate the difference between  $*d'$  and  $*d'_1$  as follows:  $*d'_1$  is posited if at least one language displays the expected reflex, otherwise  $*d'$  will be reconstructed. One unpleasant consequence of such a reconstruction is brought about by the ambiguous character of  $d'$  in Galla, Konso, and Gidole. In cases where all three languages display a  $d'$  reflex of  $*d'_1$  — and the amount of confusion described above would seem to indicate that we must reckon with such cases — our reconstruction would nevertheless indicate  $*d'$ . It would thus be a false reconstruction, unless some other language(s) could be found that provide(s) evidence for disambiguation.

Let us now consider Galla  $t'$ . We can find at least two instances of Galla  $t'$  corresponding to Konso  $j$ :

Galla  $k'urt'umm-ii$  'fish'        = Konso  $murkuuj-a$

Galla  $t'ur$-  'be dirty'          = Konso  $jur-eeta$  'dirt'

If *k'urt'ummii* is related to Somali *kalluun* (< *kalluum*) 'id.', as is generally assumed, the sequence *ll* in Somali could be taken to result from assimilation. The glottalized *k'* in Galla is clearly secondary, it is caused by assimilation to *t'* (distance assimilation as in numerous other cases of secondary glottalization in Galla). The Gidole cognate of *k'urt'ummii* is *murkudd'-a* 'tadpole, fish', another instance of Konso *j* versus Gidole *d'*. The correspondence

$$\text{Gidole } d' \qquad = \text{ Konso } j \qquad = \text{ Galla } t'$$

can again be taken to represent the reflexes of a further proto-phoneme $*d'_3$, but the evidence is too scanty to allow for solid conclusions. For the present, Galla *t'* is best considered to be an irregular reflex of $*d'_1$, and the word for 'fish' will thus be reconstructed as $*murkuud'_1-$ (and, by metathesis, $*kurd'_1uum-$).

As already stated, both *d'* and $*d'_1$ correspond to Afar, Somali, Boni, Rendille, Dasenech, Arbore and Elmolo *d'* (*ɗ*). Examples were given above; the following are some further cognate sets showing the reflexes of $*d'_1$:

$*d'_1ak'-/*d'_1ik'-$ 'wash': Som. *ɗaq-*, Rend. *ɗix-*, (Das. *g'ik-?*).

$*d'_1uf-$ 'close, shut': Som. *juf-* .

$*d'_1i(i)f-$ 'grow tall, stretch oneself': Som. *jiif-* 'stretch oneself, lie down'.

$*d'_1ifr-$ 'braid': Rendille *ɗafar*, Dasenech *dafarri* 'clothes', and perhaps also Saho *-dful-* (pref.) 'plait'.

$*d'_1iib-$ 'squeeze, press': Som. *ɗiidiib-* (intens.) 'bring thighs together to close crutch'.

$*fuud'_1-$ 'whistle': Somali *food-*, Boni *foor-* (*d'* regularly → *r/V___V*).

$*mid'_1-$ 'fruit': Som. *mid-o*.

Cf. also Konso *jik-* 'stick something into the ground etc.' = Somali *ɗeg-* 'stick', Konso *jir-* 'remove remaining e.g. porridge in gourd with the edge of the pointer finger (and similar actions)' = Som. *dur-* 'scoup up'. The Somali *j* reflex in the words for 'close' and 'stretch', although irregular, seems to support the reconstruction of a proto-phoneme distinct from *d'*. It may thus tentatively be assumed that other instances of Somali *j* versus *d'* in other languages can also be explained as resulting from $*d'_1$, e.g. Som. *qanjid* 'lymphatic gland' = Konso *qand'-itta* (or perhaps *qand'id'-ta?*) 'udder; swollen or abnormally big "gland" (esp. on back of neck)'.

We have yet to examine possible reflexes of *d'* and $*d'_1$ in HEC, Dullay, and Yaaku.

HEC is not uniform as to the number of glottalized consonants in the denti-alveolar region. All members seem to possess a phoneme *t'* which continues both *d'* and $*d'_1$:

Sid., Kamb., Al., Had. *t'ibb-e* 'hundred' = Galla *d'ibb-a*, Konso *d'ipp-a*, Gidole *d'ipp* (PEC *d'ibb-*).

Sid., Had. *t'ur-* 'be dirty' = Galla *t'ur-*, Konso *jur-* (PEC $*d'_1ur-$).

Some HEC languages such as Hadiyya appear not at all to possess a voiced *d'*. There is, however, a reflex *ʾ* in some words in positions where medial *t'* would be expected. Sidamo does indeed show *d'* in such cases, and it may be assumed that Proto-HEC medial *t'* became *d'* in certain environments, and that the latter continues as Hadiyya *ʾ* and as Sidamo,

Darasa etc. *d'*.  In Sidamo and Darasa this original allophonic distribution was obscured
by heavy borrowing from Galla, or rather, by a tendency to make Sidamo words similar in
form to the corresponding Galla words.  Sidamo *t'* is nearly always retained as such, if
there is no corresponding Galla item: *t'am²-* 'ask' = Hadiyya *t'a²m-*; *t'o²-* 'extinguish'
= Hadiyya *t'o²-* etc.; however, *t'eer-to* ~ *d'eer-to* 'long' = Galla *d'eer-*; *t'ib-* ~ *d'ib-*
'narrow' = Galla *d'ib-* etc.

All HEC languages have a phoneme *c'* which is mainly confined to loanwords.  The two or
three instances in which it appears to be autochthonous do not seem to have cognates outsid
HEC.

Fortunately both Dullay and Yaaku seem to separate *$*d'$* and *$*d'_1$* (or even more *$*d'$*'s) quite
nicely.  Both languages distinguish three relevant phonemes, *d'*, *t'*, and *c'*.  The latter
has a reflex *k'* in the Gawwada and Gollango dialects of Dullay, but this may be a later
development resulting from depalatalization.  Yaaku *t'* is said to be pronounced as an
an affricate *ts'* (Heine 1975:36) and so is *t'* in at least some varieties of
Dullay (notably in Gollango).  Heine's transcription of Yaaku *d'* as *d'* is a purely
orthographic device.  Dullay *d'* corresponds to *$*d'$*, as in Harso *d'iš-* 'plant' (<
*$*d'iš-$*), *hund'ur-ce* 'navel' (< *$*hund'ur-$*), *d'iic-* 'kick' (< *$*d'iit-$*), *d'al-* 'give birth'
(< *$*d'al-$*).  The Yaaku reflexes of these words are *dis-*, *hendero*, *diit-*, and *del-*.  There
is no known instance of a *d'* word in Yaaku, for which a proto-form with *$*d'_1$* would have
to be posited on the evidence of some other language.  In general this would also appear
to be true of Dullay, with the exception that there are three contradictory cases, which
merit some discussion.  The first one is Gawwada *d'ixil-xo* 'elbow' cited by Black (1976).
However, since other varieties of Gawwada have *t'ixil-xo* , and all other Dullay dialects
uniformly display a stem *t'ihil-*/*t'ixil-*, the occurrence of *d'* in this particular Gawwada
word must be attributed to the influence of the neighboring Konsoid dialects with which
the Gawwada are in close contact.  This must also be the case with the second irregularity
*d'ilħ-e* 'charcoal', which cannot as such have been borrowed from Konsoid because of the
*ħ*, but may of course have been approximated to the Konsoid form.  The third and final
irregularity is seen in the following cognate set:

Somali *doob-o* 'mud', *doob-* 'smear mud on wall, house', Rendille *dob* 'mud', *dou-* 'paint',
Boni *d'oob-e'* 'mud', *d'ob-* 'smear'; Galla *d'oob-* 'smear mud on house or wall', Konso
*d'oop-* 'put a clump of semisolid material (e.g. dung) on wall', Gidole *d'opp-* 'make a
ball of soil, dough etc.'; Dullay (at least Dobase ) *d'oop-* 'form clay, make a pot (pot-
ter)'; as against Yaaku *t'a²p-ais-* 'to glue'.  Since the Dobase word belongs to a highly
specialized lexical stratum (that of craftsman terminology), which is on the whole
susceptible of borrowing, the occurrence of *d'* in this example should not be overestimated.

PEC *$*d'_1$* corresponds to both *t'* and *c'* in Yaaku and Dullay.  The amount of evidence is
small but consistent.  Except for one or two cognate sets which may have been overlooked,
the following is an exhaustive list of *$*d'_1$* reflexes found in the available Dullay and
Yaaku materials:

| PEC | | Dullay | | Yaaku | |
|---|---|---|---|---|---|
| *$*d'_1ak'-$*/*$*d'_1ik'-$* | 'wash' | - - | | *t'ɔq-* | |
| *$*d'_1iib-$* | 'press' | *t'iip-* | | - - | |
| *$*d'_1ikl-$* | 'elbow' | *t'ihil-* | | *t'okl-e'* | 'forearm' |
| *$*d'_1ilħ-$* | 'charcoal' | (*d'ilħ-e*) | | *t'eeh-o* | |
| *$*d'_1ookk'-$* | 'mud' | *c'ooqq-o* | | - - | |
| *$*d'_1ub-$* | 'dip in'[14] | *t'up-* | 'swim' | *t'oob-* | 'sift'? |

---

[14]Galla *c'up'-*/*c'ub-* 'dip in'.

| *d'₁uɓ- | 'close' | c'up- | | – – | |
| *d'₁uɾ- | 'dirty' | t'uɾ- | | t' ɾ- | 'bad' |
| *ʃald'₁- | 'log' | – – | | piɫc' | 'small sticks of firewood' |
| *k'ad'₁- | 'cut | qatt'- | 'cut, hoe up, fold' | qat'- | |
| *muɾkuud'₁-/*kuɾmuud'₁- | 'fish' | muɾkuut'-o, kuɾmuut'-o | | | |

As expected in view of the inconsistent treatment of *d'₁ in Galla, Konso, and Gidole noted earlier, we find instances of *d'₁ in Dullay and/or Yaaku which correspond to an apparent *d' in Macro-Oromo. Dullay and/or Yaaku may thus serve to disambiguate. One such instance is Dullay *t'iiɾ-akko* 'man, male', for which Galla, Konso, and Gidole display the root *d'iiɾ-*, but which may nevertheless be set up as *d'₁iiɾ- on the basis of the Dullay evidence.

If there were regular correspondences between Yaaku *c'* and Dullay *c'* on the one hand, and Yaaku *t'* and Dullay *t'* on the other, a good case could be made for a third proto-phoneme, and the following hypothesis could be maintained for the development of PEC glottalized sounds in the denti-alveolar region:

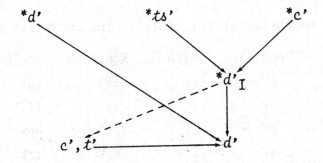

Unfortunately, no such evidence is as yet available. The explanation of the double representation of *d'₁ as both *t'* and *c'* must therefore be left to future research.

## 4.16.   PEC *s AND *š

In previous papers (Sasse 1975, 1976) I tried to demonstrate that PEC had at least two voiceless sibilants, symbolized as *s and *š. The reconstruction of these phonemes was done almost exclusively on the basis of Galla which was said to reflect *s and *š in the form of ʃ and s, respectively. We will see below that the actual situation is somewhat more complicated than this.

In nearly all other languages the two sibilants merged into s. Only Somali (+ Boni and Rendille), Konso, and Gidole provide restrictive indications of *š. Burji, which was taken to show some random preservations of š in Sasse (1975), can now be analyzed as shifting s (regardless of whether from *s or *š) to š after i.[15] The same rule is apparently valid for Dasenech.

---

[15] One or two unexpected preservations of initial š must then result from borrowing.

In some southern Somali varieties (Jiddu, Ašraf) intervocalic *š* remained as such, whereas in northern Somali, "Jabarti", and Boni intervocalic *š* became *y*. In Rendille the regular reflex seems to be *c*. It can be assumed (Heine 1978b) that Proto-Somali-Boni Rendille had a phoneme \*c which itself originated from the merger of the palatalized reflexes of PEC \*k and preservations of intervocalic *š*. This \*c continues as *š* initially and as *y* mediall\* in Somali and Boni, as *š* in all positions in Ašraf and Jiddu, and remained unchanged in all positions in Rendille. Since Proto-Somali-Boni-Rendille \*c continues intervocalic \*š only when root-internal, it can be assumed that root-final \*š must have been subject to analogical leveling for some reason. A very plausible reason is seen in the fact that a regular morphophonemic alternation between *s* and *š* has been operating in the ancestor of these languages. Before we turn to this alternation, we have to examine the reflexes of \*š in Konso and Gidole. In Konso PEC \*š seems to continue as *s* except after *i*, *y*, and *r*, where it remained as such. In Gidole it became *yy* in the same environments except after *r*. It has already been shown in Sasse (1975) that it is not possible to consider *š* as a secondary development after *i*, unless one assumes the great number of words with the sequence -*is*- has entered Konso by the way of borrowing. But the fact that Gidole has *s* where Konso has *s*, and *yy* where Konso has *š* is sufficient confirmation for the originality of Konsoid \*

Morphophonemic rules which led to the merger of \**s* and \**š* were already present in PEC. Sir no *š*C sequence is reconstructable for PEC, and since there are alternations between *š* befor V and *s* before C, it can be concluded that PEC had a fairly general rule of the form

$$š \rightarrow s \ / \ \underline{\hspace{1em}} \ C$$

One of the most striking examples for the operation of this rule is the causative paradigm:

| | PEC | North-Som./Boni | Jiddu | Rendille | Galla | Konso | Gidole |
|---|---|---|---|---|---|---|---|
| 1s | -*šV* | -*yV* | -*šV* | -*cV* | -*sV* | -*šV* | -*yyV* |
| 2s | -*stV* | -*sV* | -*stV* | -*sV* | -*ſtV* | -*ssV* | -*ttV* |
| 3sm | -*šV* | -*yV* | -*šV* | -*cV* | -*sV* | -*šV* | -*yyV* |
| 3sf | -*stV* | -*sV* | -*stV* | -*sV* | -*ſtV* | -*ssV* | -*ttV* |
| 1p | -*snV* | -*nV* | -*snV* | -*nV* | -*ſnV* | -*nnV* | -*nnV* |
| 2p | -*stVnV* | -*sVn* | -*stVn* | -*sVn* | -*ſtVnV* | -*ssVn* | -*ttVnV* |
| 3p | -*šVnV* | -*yVn* | -*šVn* | -*cVn* | -*sVnV* | -*šVn* | -*yyVnV* |

What has been said up to now is, with minor modifications, the state of affairs as presente in Sasse (1975, 1976). Independent evidence for \**s* and \**š* has since then come from the Dullay languages. PEC sibilants as reconstructed on the evidence of Galla, Konso etc. were almost always found to be isomorphic with those found in the Dullay cognates.

Examples for PEC \**s*:

PEC \**saal*- 'cow-dung', as reconstructed from Somali *saal-o*, Konso *saal*- vs. Galla *ſaal*-, is properly represented as *sal-te* in Dullay (Gollango).

PEC \**sorn*- 'nasal mucus', as reconstructed from e.g. Konso *sorn-eeta* vs. Galla *ſurr-ii*, is properly represented as Harso *surun-ho*.

PEC \**sun(u)n*- 'nose-bleeding', as reconstructed from e.g. Dasenech *suun-a* and Galla *ſunun-*, is properly represented as Harso *sunun-ho*.

PEC \**bis*- 'color, flower', as reconstructed from Afar *bis-u*, Konso *pis-a* vs. Galla *biſ-a*, i properly represented as Dullay *pis-akko*.

Examples for PEC *š:

PEC *šeeb- 'leather strap', as reconstructed from e.g. Dasenech seeb vs. Galla seep'-ani, is confirmed by Harso šeep-akko 'leather belt'.

PEC *šok'- 'beat, hit', as reconstructed from e.g. Hadiyya sukk'- vs. Galla sok'- 'weed, cut off', is confirmed by Dullay šoq- 'hit'.

PEC *warš- 'rhinoceros', as reconstructed from e.g. Konso orš-ayta and Galla wors-eesa, is confirmed by Dullay orš-.

PEC *d'iš- 'build, plant', as reconstructed from e.g. Somali dis- 'build' vs. Galla d'is- 'stretch skin out' and Konso d'iš- 'plant', is confirmed by Dullay d'iš- 'plant'.

Other examples for PEC *s = Galla ɓ, Dullay s and for PEC *š = Galla s, Dullay š include: Galla gaaɓ-a, Dullay kaas-s-o 'horn' (PEC *gaas-), Galla gaɓar-sa, Dullay kasar-ko 'buffalo' (PEC *gasar-); Galla sor-, Dullay šor- 'rich' (PEC *šor-), Galla saal-a, Gollango šal-to 'oryx' (PEC *šaal-). A nice example of both *s and *š occurring in the same word is Harso ošoᶜs- = Galla suuɓ- (< *šuᶜs-) 'smell'.

On the basis of this new evidence one suspects that *s does not always become ɓ in Galla:

Dullay sapsap- 'spider' (= 'deceiver'): Galla sabab-, Somali sassab- etc. 'deceive'.

Dullay sipil-ho 'metal': Galla sibiil-a 'id.'

Dullay (Harso) sip-te 'mud': Galla sup'-ee 'id.'

Dullay samay-ho 'spear-shaft': Galla soomay-a 'id.'

With the exception of 'metal', these words do not look like loanwords. They all have, however, one thing in common, namely, the consonant next to s is a labial. We can therefore assume that *s did not become ɓ before a labial.

A second set of exceptions comprises the following irregular correspondences:

Gollango sok-o 'son-in-law': Galla sodd-a '...-in-law', Somali soddog, soddoh 'father-, mother-in-law', Dasenech suoz- '...-in-law'.

Dullay isseh, essah 'three': Galla sadii etc.

Both of these cognate sets have in common that they involve a sequence *s/šVz..., and the irregularities may have been caused by this unusual sequence.

We may now proceed to the listing of the entire set of regular reflexes of PEC *s and *š, which is given in the table below.

|       |              | Af | So | Re | Bo | Ar | Da | El | Ba | Ga | Ko | Gi | HEC | Bu | Du | Ya |
|-------|--------------|----|----|----|----|----|----|----|----|----|----|----|-----|----|----|----|
| *s    | normally in  | s  | s  | s  | s  | s  | s  | s  | s  | ɓ  | s  | s  | s   | s  | s  | s  |
|       | certain env. |    | i  |    |    |    | š  |    |    | s  |    |    |     | š  |    | h  |
| *š    | normally in  | s  | s  | s  | s  | s  | s  | s  | s  | s  | s  | s  | s   | s  | š  | s  |
|       | certain env. |    | y  | c  | y  | ?  | y  | ?  |    |    | š  | yy |     | š  |    |    |

"In certain environments" for š in Somali, Rendille, Boni, Dasenech, Konso and Gidole is meant as defined above. In Burji, s becomes š after i. Two morphophonemic alternations in individual languages have not yet been discussed: In Boni, s becomes i (or rather y) before consonants, as in *kas-a* 'I know': *kei-ta* 'you know'. The second form should perhaps better be written /*kayta*/. In the same environment, and apparently also word-finally, Yaaku *s* becomes *h*: *kus-aa* vs. *kuh-taa*, *depih* vs. *deps-*.

There are two cases in which the Dullay dialects obviously show irregular *s* reflexes of PEC *š. The first one is the stem of the third person personal pronoun, and the other one is the causative morpheme. Since from the analysis presented so far it has emerged that the Dullay dialects preserved *s* and *š* better than any other EC language, inconsistencies in these two basic items merit detailed discussion. Let us take up the personal pronouns first.

The Dullay forms of the third person pronouns are m. *uso* 'he', f. *ise* 'she', and pl. *usuno*, *isino*, *usund'e*, *isind'e* according to dialect. These are inconsistent with my reconstruction m. *ˀuš-*, f. *ˀiš-* as proposed and motivated in Sasse 1975. It is appropriate at this point to reconsider the relevant facts which led to this reconstruction.

The reconstruction of *š in the roots of the 3rd person pronouns was based on the observation that Konso displays a consistent stem /iš-/ in all three forms:

    m.   *iš-a*

    f.   *iš-ee-nna*

    pl.  *iš-oo-nna*

By comparing this with Galla

    m.   *is-a*

    f.   *is-ii* (dial. *iš-ii*)

    pl.  *is-aani*

which because of their *s* equally point to *š, I came to the conclusion that the PEC starred forms for the 3rd person pronouns are best set up with an *š. Being in the initial stages of my reconstructive work at that time, I overlooked the fact that such a reconstruction would render difficult, if not impossible, the explanation of the Somali forms

    m.   *is-a*

    f.   *iy-a*

    pl.  *iy-o*

It has already been observed by Moreno (1951) and was repeated by Heine (1978b), that in Northern Somali *š (Heine's *c) became *y* intervocalically. *isa* must thus be *ˀisa*, while *iya* may perhaps go back to *iš-a* (cf. below for a slightly different explanation). Since other EC languages offer no evidence for either *s* or *š*, we have to confine ourselves to these contradictory forms, and try to find the best hypothesis to account for the irregularities.

It seems most plausible now to attribute the m. -*s*- vs. f. -*š*- dichotomy in Somali not to internal irregular development, but to the original PEC distribution of *s* and *š* in the pronominal forms. This is confirmed by Rendille m. *usu*, f. *ice*, and Boni *us^u*, f. *ii* (< *iyi*). We have thus to reconstruct

    m.  *ˀus-uu* (perhaps accusative *ˀus-aa*)

    f.  *ˀiš-ii* (perhaps accusative *ˀiš-ee*)

It is obvious that the shapes in which the personal pronouns present themselves in the modern EC languages are the result of heavy analogical restructuring. The different vocalism (*u* vs. *i*) is now found only in Saho-Afar (*usuk* vs. *ise*), in the Dullay dialects, and in the Boni and Rendille forms cited above, but it was certainly the original one. For all the remaining EC languages a generalization of the *i*-variant must be assumed. In some cases the feminine stem as a whole came to form the basis of all 3rd person pronouns (as in Oromoid), in other cases the generalization covered only the vocalism, while the consonantal distinction between masculine and feminine/plural was maintained (as in Somali). Moreover, it can be assumed that the original feminine form in Somali was *iyi* rather than *iya* (as Boni still has *ii* from *iyi*), and that the latter owes its final vowel to the analogy of the masculine form *isa*.

It can be concluded, then, that Dullay *us-o* 'he' is the regular reflex of PEC *ʔus-uu, while earlier *ʔiš-ee was restructured to *is-e* on the model of *uso*. The personal pronouns do not therefore contribute any counterevidence to the assumption that Dullay regularly continues *s and *š as such.

Quite similar arguments are valid for the causative morpheme, which occurs as -Vs- in Dullay, although the original PEC form reconstructed from the evidence of Somali, Galla, Gidole, Konso etc. must be posited as *-(i)š-. The explanation for this apparent discrepancy is not hard to find; it is derivable from the reconstructed PEC causative paradigm given in the table on page 32 above. Both *š* and *s* already occurred as morphophonemic alternants in PEC. It should not come as a surprise that this kind of alternation is eradicated by paradigm analogy.

One final remark on possible objections against the phonemic status of PEC *š may be in order. Since most of the apparent preservations of *š* seem to occur after *i* or *y*, one may legitimately ask whether *š should not be regarded as a secondary development, at least allophonic in PEC, or perhaps even independently created in some of the individual languages. There are several minimal pairs which go aginst such an explanation, the most obvious being the following:

PEC *ʔis- 'self, oneself', a reflexive pronoun, which continues as Afar *is-i*, Somali and Rendille *is*, Boni *se* (< *is-e*); Elmolo *is*, Galla *uɟ-i*, Konso *is-i*, Gidole *iss*; Yaaku *eh*.

PEC *ʔiš-, the stem of the 3sf personal pronoun, which continues as Saho *is-e*; Somali *iy-a*, Rendille *ic-e*, Boni *ii*, Elmolo *is-e*, Baiso *is-ee*; Galla *is-ii*, Konso *iš-ee-nna*; HEC *is-ee*; and Yaaku *is-i*.

## 4.17.  PEC *ħ AND *ᶜ

PEC possessed two pharyngeal fricatives, a voiceless *ħ and a voiced *ᶜ. The latter was presumably preglottalized (i.e. it was something like a pharyngeal affricate ʔᶜ), since it is still so pronounced in those EC languages that preserve this phoneme, and its development into ʔ (glottal stop) in the remaining languages also suggests that a certain amount of glottalization accompanied the realization of the proto-phoneme.

The PEC pharyngeals are preserved as such in Saho-Afar, Somali, Rendille, and in the Dullay languages. Rendille *ᶜ* is currently in the process of merging with *ħ* (Heine 1975: 187). The following comparisons demonstrate this regular correspondence:

PEC *ħizk-/*ħuzk- 'star': Saho-Afar *ħutuk*, Somali *ħiddig*, Dullay *ħisk-e*.

PEC *ᶜal- 'mountain, highland': Saho *ᶜal* 'mountain', Somali *ᶜal* 'any lofty, coastal range of mountains', Rendille *ħal* 'mountain', Dullay *ᶜal-e* 'mountain, highland'.

PEC *malħ- 'pus': Saho *malaħ*, Somali *malaħ*, Dullay *malaħ-te*.

PEC *gan<sup>ᶜ</sup>- '(palm of) hand': Afar gena<sup>ᶜ</sup>-ta, Somali ga<sup>ᶜ</sup>an, Dullay kana<sup>ᶜᶜ</sup>-e.

In HEC, Burji, Macro-Oromo, Yaaku, and the remainder of the Omo-Tana group the pharyngeals merged with the glottals h and, ', respectively. These are generally well preserved in Boni and Yaaku, where ᶜ continues as ' and ħ as h in all positions, as can be seen from the following examples taken from Heine (1974, 1978a). Note that Heine does not write initial '.

*ħizk- 'star': Boni hidde', Yaaku hinso' (pl.).

*malħ- 'pus': Yaaku milɛh.

*gan<sup>ᶜ</sup>- '(palm of) hand': Boni ka'an, Yaaku kinne', pl. ki'n-ɛi.

*d'amħ- 'cold': Boni d'ahan, Yaaku dɛhmo.

*k'uɓa<sup>ᶜ</sup>- 'cough': Boni uɓa'-, Yaaku qopɛ'ɛ-.

*<sup>ᶜ</sup>arrab- 'tongue': Boni arub, Yaaku ɛrɛ.

In Baiso, Arbore, Dasenech, Elmolo, and Yaaku a was raised to e (sometimes also i) in the environment of pharyngeals prior to their merger with h and ', so that in some cases pharyngeals may be internally reconstructed from the vocalism in these languages (cf. Sasse (1973), Heine (1978b), and Sasse (forthcoming)). The word for 'tongue' just cited is an example: Baiso irreb-i, Dasenech 'ere, Elmolo ɛrrep. Other examples of this change include:

*<sup>ᶜ</sup>al- 'mountain': Arbore el, Elmolo ɛl 'stone'.

*ka<sup>ᶜ</sup>- 'stand up': Dasenech ke'-, Elmolo kɛ'-, Yaaku kɛ'ɛ.

*matħ- 'head': Baiso mɛte, Arbore mete, Dasenech me, Elmolo mɛtɛ', Yaaku mitɛh.

In Baiso *ħ seems to continue as h (hididi 'root' = PEC *ħizz-, lɛh 'six' = PEC *lih-), whereas *ᶜ is generally lost (meege 'name' = PEC *mag<sup>ᶜ</sup>-). In Arbore and Elmolo h and ' are sometimes retained and sometimes lost; unfortunately the paucity of the data does not allow for any conclusion as to what the exact conditioning factors are. In Dasenech, on the other hand, the situation is quite clear: ᶜ and ħ regularly continue as ' and h word-initially (*<sup>ᶜ</sup>azz- 'white' → 'ez; *ħid'- 'tie' → hiz/t-); in all other positions ħ and of course also h is dropped, and so is ᶜ, except word-finally where the latter appears as ' (*ša<sup>ᶜ</sup>- 'cow' → se').

*ħ generally appears as h and *ᶜ as ' (optionally zero) in Macro-Oromo and HEC, provided that they are not flanked by a consonant. In certain Konsoid varieties, including the Konso dialect I am familiar with, intervocalic, ' disappeared leaving a vowel cluster which is generally resolved by a semivowel (y or w according to the vocalic environment): Konso *le'a → lea → leʸa 'moon' (PEC *le<sup>ᶜ</sup>-).

Both *ħ and *ᶜ (i.e. h and ') disappear and simultaneously cause compensatory lengthening of the preceding or following vowel in Galla when adjacent to consonants: *matħ-a 'head' → mat-aa, *d'aħl- 'inherit' → d'aal-, *ge<sup>ᶜ</sup>l- 'love' → jaal-, *gan<sup>ᶜ</sup>-a 'palm of hand' → gan-aa. The same process is found in Konso and HEC, but is operative only BEFORE consonants. After consonants pharyngeals are simply deleted without compensatory lengthening of the following vowel in both languages, as in *malħ-a → Konso mal-a, Hadiyya mar-a 'pus'. In Gidole, h and ' are generally well preserved when adjacent to consonants, except that h is fully assimilated to a preceding consonant (obligatorily to obstruents, as in matħ-a → mašš(-a), optionally to sonorants, as in malħ(-a) ~ mall(-a). In some cases, such assimilation was also observed in Konso, as in *sesh-a 'three' → sessa, math-a 'head'* → *matt-a*, so perhaps distinct behavior of obstruents and sonorants is also involved here.

An interesting isogloss which pertains to the behavior of ʾ after coronal sonorants separates one Gidole variety from the other.  In the Gidole dialect described by Black, ʾ appears as *d'* after *ℓ*, *ɾ*, and *n*, whereas my own data indicate the regular ʾ reflex in the same position: Black *keɾd'-*, Sasse *keɾʾ-* 'become old' (possibly from a root *geɾᶜ-*, cf. Galla *jaaɾ-sa* < *geᶜɾ-ita*).

Initial *h* (regardless of whether from *ħ* or from *h*) is relatively unstable in Galla and HEC and perhaps less so in other languages.  Black (personal communication) assumes that in Galla *h* became zero while Galla *h* continues PEC *ħ*. This is, however, contradicted by forms such as *uɾj-ii* 'star' (besides the rare *huɾj-ii*) < PEC *ħuzk-*, and *hal-aa* 'she-camel' < PEC *hal-*.  Further examples of Galla *h* < PEC *ħ* will be given in 4.18.

There are occasional instances of pharyngeal loss in languages that would normally otherwise preserve these sounds.  Only one such case is known from Dullay: *ayy-akkφ* 'locust' vs. Somali *ayaħ* 'id.', a unique irregularity which I am not at present able to explain.

In Saho-Afar and Somali, however, pharyngeal loss is so common that it is worthwhile speculating about a possible explanation.

The most conspicuous cases in Somali are the following:

*siddeed* 'eight' vs. *saddeħ* 'three'.

*mud-* 'prick, stab' vs. *mudaᶜ* 'fork' (originally 'bodkin').

*waɾan* 'spear' vs. Dullay *oɾħan-ko* 'id.', Galla *woɾaan-a* (= *waɾφan-a*) 'id.', Rendille *waɾħan* 'knife'.

*šab-eeℓ* 'leopard' vs. Afar *kabeᶜ* 'id.'.

*ɖam-* 'complete' vs. Rendille *d'axan* (probably misheard for *d'aħan*) 'all', Gidole *d'ahenn* 'all'.

*ᶜiidan = midiidin* 'servant'.

*ɓaℓ-* 'bewitch' vs. Saho (pref.) *-ɓᶜiℓ-* 'meditate, think up, hatch'.

Most of these irregularities can be explained by assuming an earlier morphophonemic rule which deleted pharyngeals after consonants.  *mudᶜ-V* thus became *mud-V*, but *mudaᶜ-* remained *mudaᶜ*.  In the same way *kebᶜ-eel → šabeeℓ*, *waɾħan → waɾan* etc.  For a case such as *ɓaℓ-* one could assume the loss of the pharyngeal to have been caused by the shape *-ɓᶜVℓ-* of the earlier prefix verb.

This explanation seems plausible, but presents difficulties in several respects.  One of the problems that I see lies in the fact that there are too many Somali words which preserve PEC sequences of consonant + pharyngeal.  This could of course be explained as caused by analogy, since for every shape CVCC we have to assume an alternant CVCVC (cf. 3.5).  We thus posit PEC *math ~ *mataħ-* 'head', and in the latter variant pharyngeal loss did of course not occur.  Moreover, when pharyngeal deletion as an automatic rule was given up, the pharyngeals were easily reintroduced into postconsonantal positions on the model of other CVCC ~ CVCVC alternations.  On the other hand, if pharyngeal deletion really were a morphophonemic rule in Somali, one would perhaps expect more fossilized variation.

There is, however, a more serious problem.  Consider the verb *ɓaℓ-*, which has several cognates outside Somali and Saho: Hadiyya ʕar- 'bewitch, deceive', Dasenech ʕal- 'lie', Galla ʕal-m- 'argue, quarrel, criticize', Rendille ʕal- 'curse', and several others. From what we know of the reflexes of pharyngeals in these languages, none of these forms can have originated in *ʕaʕl- (this should become Hadiyya ʕaar-, Dasenech ʕel-, Galla ʕaal- etc.). In other words, all these forms go back to a PEC variant *ʕal- without a pharyngeal. This would seem to indicate that something like the pharyngeal deletion rule posited above for Somali dates back to a much earlier stage. That this may actually be the case is also suggested by some instances of pharyngeal loss in Saho-Afar:

mud- 'stab', cf. Som. mud- above.

ʕaan (Reinisch, the long vowel is not reliable) 'space, interval' = Somali ʕanaħ 'gap between front incisors', Rendille ʕahan 'gap in upper teeth ridge' < PEC *ʕanħ-. HEC ʕan- 'open' is obviously cognate, but does not contribute to the problem under discussion.

Both instances clearly indicate pharyngeal loss in postconsonantal position. But if we were to accept the version of a pan-PEC pharyngeal deletion rule, it would be impossible to account for retentions of postconsonantal pharyngeals such as Rendille warhan and Dullay orhan-ko, which occur MORPHEME-INTERNALLY without the slightest possibility for any morphophonemic alternation that could support such retention. Clearly something must be wrong with this hypothesis, but I am unable at present to say what a more plausible solution would look like.

A quite different kind of pharyngeal loss in Saho-Afar can be seen in the following comparisons:

um-a 'bad' vs. Som. ħun (ħum-), Galla ham-aa (PEC *ham-/*ħum-).

-olool- 'graze (of cattle' vs. Som. ʕalaal- 'chew the cud'.

-oɗʼ-'tie' vs. Som. ħiɗ-.

Black (1974) suggests that the adjacency to back vowels may play a role in pharyngeal loss in Saho-Afar. This is in fact confirmed by internal evidence, e.g. -oɗʼ- 'tie' cited above, as compared with -idħiɗ- 'sew' from the same root -ħ-ɗ-.

## 4.18.  PEC *h

In Black (1974) *h is reconstructed in a very limited number of cases. One finds seven instances of initial *h, and two clear and one problematic instance of medial *h. Initial *h is said to yield Som. h, Saho zero before u, h elsewhere, and Galla, Konso, and Gidole zero. However, the inspection of further cognate sets and even a thorough examination of Black's reconstructions indicate that the situation is much more complicated than this. Only four of the seven cognate sets given by Black really show the zero reflex in Galla:

*hebel- 'what's-his-name': Saho hebel-a (spelled "habel-ā" by Reinisch), Som. hebel, Galla ebel-uu (dial. abal-uu).

*hurguʄ- 'shake off': Saho urguʄ-, Som. hurguʄ-, Galla urguʄ-.

*hub- 'know, be sure': Som. hub-, Galla ub-adʼ/t-, Konso and Gidole up-.

*huww- 'dress, wear': Som. huw-ad- 'drape self in a garment', Wollega Galla uww-is- (caus.) 'cover, dress', Konso and Gidole uww-adʼ/t- 'wear'.

Of the three remaining reconstructions, *haay- 'hold' (Somali haay-, Saho hay- 'put'),
and *haɓɓ- 'drown' (Som. haɓ-t- (refl.), Konso aɓɓ- 'smother') have no known Galla cognates, whereas *ha 'jussive particle' (Som. ha, Konso a) appears as Galla ha. Moreover,
for uɾguɓ- 'shake off' and ub-ad'/t- 'know', da Thiene (1939) gives the shapes huɾguɓ-
and hub-ad'/t-. The following four comparisons not included in Black (1974) also appear
to show an h reflex of PEC *h in Galla:

*hal- 'she-camel': Som. hal (Bell), Rendille al-o (sg. ay-u), Galla hal-aa. If Saho
al-a (pl. of lah 'female goat') is a cognate, it would show a zero reflex of PEC *h before
a.

*hamhaam- 'yawn': Som. hamaan-s-t- (caus. refl.), Rend. amaa-s-t- (caus. refl.), Boni
hamaam-s-t- (caus. refl.), Galla hamoom-ad'/t- (refl.).

*hagoog- 'cover the head with a cloth': Saho agoog- 'be covered with cloths, draped in
garments'; Somali hagog 'cloth draped over the head', Rendille ogog- 'cover', Galla
hagoog-ad'/t-.

*haɾ- 'pond, creek': Saho aɾ-a 'river, creek', Som. haɾ-o lake', Arbore haɾ-u 'river',
Galla haɾ-oo 'swamp', Konso haaɾ-ta 'artificial pond, reservoir', Gidole haɾ-tot 'reservoir'.

On the basis of these examples one could hypothesize that Galla regularly preserves *h at
least before a. But this is contradicted by huɾguɓ- ~ uɾguɓ- 'shake' cited above, and
also by the following cognate set:

*habaaɾ- 'curse': Saho abaaɾ-, Som. habaaɾ-, Boni habaaɾ-, Rend. abaaɾ-, Galla abaaɾ-.

We have to conclude, then, that Galla h is, to say the least, unstable in initial position
and that both h and zero can consequently reflect PEC *h, regardless of the quality of the
following vowel. The question that now arises is whether only PEC *h yields unstable
h's in Galla, or all initial h's are unstable regardless of whether they derive from *h
or from *ħ. That the latter is in fact the case can easily be concluded from the available
material. Da Thiene cites e.g. "anduɾa" and "handuɾa" ((h)and'uuɾa) 'navel', "aɾɾe"
and "haɾɾe" ((h)aɾɾee) 'donkey', and he has "huɾgi" 'star' while other sources including
the most reliable ones have only uɾjii. All these words are definitely known to go back
to PEC forms with initial *ħ, *ħand'uɾ-, *ħaɾɾ-, and *ħuzk-, respectively. Cf. also
Moreno (1939:27): "h spesso scompare, specialmente in posizione intervocalica. Es. *iɾiyâ*,
compagno, per *hiɾiyâ*.". There is therefore nothing to suggest that PEC *h and *ħ received
any distinct treatment in Galla.

At first blush, the zero and h reflexes of h do not seem to be more regularly distributed
in Saho-Afar than they are in Galla. We have three zero reflexes before a, one before u,
and one h reflex each before e and a. The following cognate set shows a zero reflex of
*h before o:

*heg-/*hog- 'be erect, stand': Som. hinj-i- (caus.) 'lift', Galla hej- ~ ej-; Saho og-,
only in derived forms og-us- (caus.) 'lift', og-ut- (refl.) 'get up'.

Another zero reflex before u is shown in Saho-Afar u(u)ɾ- 'recover from illness', Sidamo
and Burji huɾ- 'id.', Som. huɾ- 'begin to burn up well (fire)' (PEC *huɾ-). It seems,
then, that in spite of the limited evidence the zero reflex of PEC *h should be regarded
as "normal" for Saho-Afar, and the h reflex shown in hebel- and hay- should be taken as
irregular. In view of this it become questionable whether Saho "hay-" (Reinisch) is at
all related to Somali haay-. There is some good evidence that Somali haay- derived from
an earlier *haaš-, or better *haš- (Andrzejewski has hay- rather than haay-), cf. Sasse
(1976). In addition to the more concrete meaning 'hold, keep', this verb originally also

denoted 'keep on doing something', and may in fact be related to Saho-Afar as- (perhaps also Sidamo os-, Hadiyya oss-) 'spend the day'. Saho "hay-", on the other hand, is probably to be interpreted as ħay- and may in fact be the suffix conjugation variant of the common verb Saho -uħu-, Afar -eħ- 'give', as Reinisch himself suggests. In Reinisch's rather unreliable transcription of Saho, ħ and h are generally not distinguished.

We have as yet found no zero reflex of *h in Somali and Boni. This may certainly be due to some circularity inherent in our arguments: if Somali and Boni are taken to be the only EC languages characterized by preservation of initial *h without exception, it is of course impossible to find zero reflexes of *h- in these two languages. Nevertheless, there could be initial h's in, say, Galla or Saho-Afar which correspond to zeroes in Somali and/or Boni. This not being the case, there is no reason at present to doubt that Somali and Boni are relatively conservative in this point. The problem just touched on demon- strates, however, that the reconstruction may involve a high degree of uncertainty, if only one or two languages out of twenty-five are taken to present evidence for a particular proto-phoneme.

As for Rendille, the normal reflex of initial *h appears to be zero. Four examples have already been cited: *hal- 'she-camel' → al-o, *hamhaam- 'yawn' → amaa-s-t-, *hagoog- 'cover' → ogog-, and *habaar- 'curse' → abaar-. Further examples which show the reflex before vowels other than a are: *hor- (Som. hor-) 'be in front' → or-, *hudr- 'sleep' (Som. hurd- by metathesis) → udur-/urd-. Only three irregularities have been noted: Som. had'- = Rend. had'- 'remain', Som. hor- 'be in front' = Rend. hor 'past' (cf. or- above), and Som. hel- = Rend. hel- 'get'. The situation in Rendille is thus similar to that in Saho-Afar.

The only example of initial *h in Dasenech is the jussive particle ha < *ha. Retention of *h is also shown in the only relevant example that the available data on the closely related Abore offer, har-u 'river' < *har-. On the other hand, Baiso has udur- AND hudur- 'sleep'.

In Konso and Gidole, *h is also not as regularly represented by zero as Black seems to believe. One example of an h reflex (PEC *har- → Konso haar-ta, Gidole har-tot) has already been given. If Konso har- 'grow weaker or poorer' is related to Rendille har- ~ ar-, Elmolo anan-ar-e 'become tired', this would constitute a further example of an h re- flex of *h, PEC *har- 'become tired or weak'.

For HEC, a regular h reflex of initial *h can be relatively safely established on the basis of comparisons such as Sid. huw-at- 'understand' < PEC *hub-, hur- 'recover from illness' < PEC *hur- (cf. also Burji hur- 'id.'), hinaas-o 'jealousy' (PEC *hinaas-, Galla hinaaʄ-a, Som. hinaas- 'emulate'). Unfortunately, initial h is very unstable in HEC, and it even appears for earlier zero in some instances such as hink'-o 'tooth' < PEC *ʾilk-. It should thus not come as a surprise that PEC *hebel- 'what's-his-name' appears as Sidamo abal-u, Had. abar-o ~ ebar-o. A further zero reflex of *h is probably also shown in Sid. ub-, Had. ubb- 'fall, raid' (Cerulli gives also Sid. hub-), if these are cognate with Som. hub 'weapons', Galla hub- 'injure'.

There is practically no evidence bearing on the fate of PEC *h in Yaaku and Dullay. If Somali and Boni are taken to be most conservative with respect to initial *h, then there is one cognate set that shows a zero reflex of *h in both Dullay and Yaaku: Somali habeen, Boni haween, Dullay awn-e 'night'; Yaaku ʾaun 'darkness'. Rendille ibeen 'night' is cognate, but displays problematic correspondences. The proto-form may have been *hawn-; the Somali, Boni, and Rendille forms go back to a different base *haween-. On the other hand, however, Yaaku has hinas- 'be jealous'.

Evidence for medial *h is quite scanty. Somali and Boni can again be taken to preserve medial *h better than other languages, but not in all environments. There is no Ch sequence

in Somali, and alternation pairs such as *iḍaah-daa* (present) vs. *iḍi* (past) 'say' suggest
that *h* was deleted after consonants: *\*iḍh-i — iḍi*, cf. Saho *eḍħe* 'id.'. This example
simultaneously shows that *\*h* adjacent to consonants was "reinforced" to yield *ħ* in Saho-
Afar. There is another example of this process: Afar *-iħdir-* 'sleep' as against the
suffix verb *\*hudr-* found in Somali, Rendille etc. The original prefix conjugation root
of this PEC verb was presumably *\*-hdir-/\*-hdur-*, from which a verbal adjective of the form
*\*hidr-/\*hudr-* was regularly derived. The latter continued as a suffix verb in Somali etc.,
as happened in numerous other cases such as *\*k'sol-* 'laugh' → *\*k'osl-*, *\*klis-/\*klus-* 'be
fat' → *\*kils-* (Somali *šilis*) etc. On the other hand, Afar *-ob-* 'hear' corresponds to PEC
*\*hub-*, so perhaps the vocalic environment also has a bearing on this.

There is one cognate set which suggests a Saho-Afar zero reflex of PEC *\*h* in intervocalic
position:

*\*bohl-* 'hole in the ground': Saho *bool* (< *bohol*); Som. *bohol*; Galla *bool-a* (< *\*bohl-a*),
Gidole *pohol-a* 'wall' (on the semantic connection between 'hole' and 'wall' cf. fn. 6);
Hadiyya *boor-a* 'salt-hole'; Dobase *pool-l-e* 'gorge'.

No instances of medial *\*h* in Elmolo, Arbore, and Baiso have been found. In Dasenech it can
be expected to yield zero on the basis of a morphophonemic rule that deletes *h* in all positions other than word-initial, and a corresponding morpheme-structure rule which allows no
medial *h*'s.

In Rendille the normal reflex of medial *\*h* is *\*ħ*:

*\*rah-* 'frog-': Som. *rah*, Rend. *raħ*.

*\*sooh-* 'plait, twist': Som. *sooh-*, Konso and Gidole *sooh-*, Rend. *soħ-*.

*\*bahal-* 'wild animal': Som. *bahal*, Rend. *baħasi* (*\*bahal-ti*) 'lion'.

*\*-d'h-* 'say': Somali *iḍaah-daa* etc., Rend. *-ḍeħ-/-ḍaħ-*.

*\*leh-* 'having': Som. *leh*, Galla *ma-lee* 'not having', Rend. *leħ-*.

The correspondence Som. *h* = Rend. *ħ* cannot, however, be absolutely taken to indicate PEC
*\*h*. We have ample evidence that at least postvocalic root-final *\*k* became *ħ* in Rendille
(naturally via *h*), as in *ilaħ*, pl. *ilk-o* 'tooth', *ḍeyeħ* (< PEC *\*d'azk-*) 'wife'[16], *luħ*
(< PEC *\*luk-*) 'foot' etc., and there is also a problematic *h* reflex of intervocalic *\*k* in
Somali (e.g. in the masculine article *-ha/-hu* from *\*-ka/-ku*).

In both Konso and Gidole intervocalic *\*h* survives as such, cf. the examples *\*sooh-* and
*\*bohl-* above. The following comparison furnishes a third example:

*\*k'ah-*: Som. *qah-* 'stampede in fear', Konso *qah-* 'flee'.

In Galla and HEC the reflexes of medial *\*h* are the same as those of *\*ħ*. It is generally
retained in intervocalic position, but disappears when adjacent to consonants or word-
final. Compensatory lengthening of the preceding vowel accompanies loss of *\*h* in both
languages: Galla *bool-a*, Had. *boor-a* < PEC *\*bohl-*; Galla *ma-lee* 'not having' < *\*ma leh*.

---

[16]This form was reconstructed as *\*d'azg-* in Sasse (1976), on the basis of Somali *daddig*
and Gidole *d'ask-itteta*. In both languages, however, *g* and *k* are ambiguous as to PEC
*\*k* or *\*g*. Then Rendille form which was unknown at that time clearly shows that *\*k* rather
than *\*g* is the original third radical.

4.19.  PEC *w AND *y

The semivowels *w and *y constitute a natural class and have consequently undergone parallel developments.  They share a tendency to merge with surrounding vowels and a further tendency to have zero reflexes in intervocalic position.  Since the evidence for PEC semivowels in initial position is less complicated, these are discussed first, before the more problematic reflexes of medial semivowels are considered.

The reflexes of PEC *w in initial position are to a considerable degree dependent on the following vowel.  There is no instance of *w before round vowels.  If there existed sequence of *wo(o)- and *wu(u)- in PEC, they have disappeared in all daughter languages and are thus irrecoverably lost.

There is one cognate set which suggests a zero reflex of *w before *e in Oromoid and Dullay:

*weger- 'olive tree' (?): Som. weger; Galla ejer-sa, Konso eker-ta, Gidole eker-r-a; Dullay eker-ko.

However, borrowing is not out of the question here, both in view of the object designated by this word and because it appears in a variety of shapes in other Ethiopian languages (Amh. wäyra, Hadiyya woᵖera etc.).  Unfortunately there is no other evidence bearing on this.

*w is regularly preserved before aa in all EC languages:

*waak'- 'sky-god': Galla waak'-a, Konso waaq-a, Das. waag (possibly borrowed, because of g), Had. waaᵖ-a, Baiso wah, Rend. wax, Elm. waak.

*waay- 'fail, be unable to be or find': Saho-Afar way-; Som. waay-; Galla waa-u 'not at all'

*waal- 'a hand-clapping game played by two teams': Som. waal-o, Galla waal-l-uu, Gidole waal-l-ayt.

No Dullay example of initial waa- has as yet been found.  For Yaaku, cf. waar- 'circulate' = Som. wareer-.

The sequence *wa- yields Saho-Afar wa-, Somali wa-, Boni wa-, Rendille wa- ~ wo-, Dasenech wo- ~ wa- (ve- before pharyngeals), Arbore wo- (we- before pharyngeals), Elmolo wa- (we- before pharyngeals), Galla wa- ~ wo-, Konso and Gidole o- (wa- before pharyngeals), Burji wa- ~ wo-, HEC wa- ~ wo-, Dullay o-.  The Yaaku reflex of initial *w is not clear.

*waᶜ- 'shout, call, invite': Saho waᶜ-; Som. waᶜ-, Rend. waħ-, Boni waᵖ-, Das. veᵖ-, Elmolo weᵖ-; Galla waa-m-; Dullay oᶜ-; Hadiyya wee-š- is probably cognate.

*war- (1) 'river': Som. war 'pool, pond', Rendille wor, Das. war, Arbore wor.

*war- (2) 'news': Saho-Afar war-e; Somali war, war-s-t- (caus. refl.) 'get news', Rendille wor-s-ad- ~ war-s-ad- 'ask'; Galla war-ee 'fame'; Sidamo wor-e 'cosa, faccenda, cosa notevole', Hadiyya wor-e 'fame'; Burji wor-s-ad'- 'ask'.

*waraab- 'draw water': Som. waraab-i- (caus.) 'to water', Rend. warab-; Galla waraab-, Konso oraap- 'fetch, dip, pour', Gidole orraap-; Yaaku irpa-.

Further examples of the o reflex in Konso-Gidole and Dullay include:  *waraab- 'hyena': Som. waraab-e, Galla waraab-esa, Konso orayta, Gid. waraab-e (with unexplained loss of b), Gawwada oraap-atte, Harso oraap-icce.  A further example of the zero reflex of initial *w in Yaaku is *wayn- (Som. weyn, Rend. ween, Boni wiin, Elm. wanyi-) 'big': Yaaku ein.

There is one example of PEC *wi-:

*wisl- 'dream': Rend. isil-l-od- (refl.), Boni wisil-l-aḍ'-(refl.), Dullay uls-.   Konso
ols- 'id.' may reflect a form with a different vocalization, PEC *wasl-.

Initial y is extremely rare.   In each EC language there are only a few words beginning
with y, and correspondences are not easy to find.   The following may be some of the relevant cases:

*yeyy-/*yoyy- 'wild dog, hunting dog, wolf': Somali yeey, Boni yeye' 'jackal'; Galla
yayy-ii, Konso yoy-ta; Sidamo (Cerulli) "iyäy"; Burji yeey-a; Dullay yoyy-akko.

*yaal-/*yeel- 'do (involuntarily)': Som. yeel- 'do, obey', yeel-sii- (caus.) 'persuade',
Rend. yel- 'make, prepare', Das. yel-m-ette (also gel-mette) (caus. refl.) 'persuade';
Konso yaal- 'work hard, strive'.

*yaad- 'think, worry': Galla yaad-, Konso yaat-; Sidamo yaad-.

*yug- 'pull off, out': Konso and Gidole yuk-; Dullay yuk-.

In the following cognate set the sequence *ye- is reflected by i in Dullay and e- in Konsoid:

*yerg- 'axe': Das. yere, pl. yerg-am, Konso erk-aha, Gidole erk-add'a, Burji yirg-a, Dullay
irk-aᶜ-o.

Intervocalic *w and *y remain as such in Konso and Gidole, Saho-Afar, Rendille, Boni, Dullay,
Burji, and apparently also in HEC.   They regularly become zero in Dasenech and Elmolo,
and alternate with zero in Galla.   In Galla, Dasenech, Rendille, and perhaps other EC languages, there is a tendency for a to become e before y and o before w.   In Arbore and in
Saho-Afar y and w seem to have been redistributed according to the surrounding vowels (this
is the first step in the direction of zero).   In Somali intervocalic y is well preserved,
but intervocalic w becomes b.   This rule came into operation after the loss of final
vowels, since w's that were intervocalic in PEC but word-final in Somali remained as such.
One example suggests that in Saho-Afar y became zero between like vowels.

Examples:

*hawaal- 'grave': Somali habaal-, Boni hawaal, Rendille hawal.

*d'aw- 'hit, strike': Elmolo d'a-, Arbore d'a-y-iy (perf.), Das. d'o-; Galla d'a(w)-,
Konso and Gidole d'aw-, Burji d'aw-.

*k'a(a)w- 'hole': Som. qaw, Galla k'a(w)a, Konso qaaw-a, Gidole k'aaw, Burji k'aw-a.

*gay- 'arrive': Afar gay-; Somali gee-y- (caus.) 'bring' (< *gay-y-, cf. below), Galla
ga(y)-, Konso kay-, Dullay o-kay-.

*nagay- 'peace, health': Saho nagaa 'peace, fortune, well-being, health' (Reinish, <
*nagay-a?), Galla nagay-a, naga·a, nagâ (underlying /nagay+a/), Konso nakay-ta 'well-being';
Dullay nakay-ho 'peace, health', nakay- 'spend the day'.

*ᵓooy- 'cry, weep': Som. ooy-, Rend. oy-, Boni oy-; Galla oo(y)-; Sidamo ooy-; Burji ooy-
'be sad'; Harso ooy-.

*kuy- 'anthill': Saho kuw-a; Galla kuy-sa, Konso kuy-ta, Gid. huy-t; Burji kuy-a; Dullay
huy-o.

There is a small amount of evidence suggesting that the sequence *-awi- became *ay already
in PEC. The normal causative derivation of the denominative verbs ending in *-a(a)w- (Saho
-aw-, Som. -aaw-, -ow-, Boni and Rendille -ow-, Galla -a(a)w-, Konso and Gidole -aaw-,
-aw-) is PEC *-ayš- (Saho -ays-, Som. -eey-, Galla -ees-, Konso -ayš-, Gidole -ayy-, Burji
-ayš- etc.). This can be assumed to derive from an earlier *-aw-iš-. One PEC root involving
the alternation -aw-/-ay- can possibly also be explained in this way: *ᶜawš-/*ᶜayš- 'grass'
(Saho-Afar ᶜays-o 'grass, straw, vegetation', Som. ᶜaws 'dry grass', Rend. hos, Baiso ees,
Das., ᵓiiš, Galla eeš 'a kind of corn', Dullay ᶜaš-ko 'grass', ᶜawš- 'become ripe', Sid.
ays-o 'grass' etc.). A hypothetical shape pre-PEC *ᶜaw(i)š- would certainly explain both
variants.[17]

The geminates PEC *ww and *yy continue as such in Macro-Oromo and Dullay (perhaps also in
HEC and Burji), and are simplified (i.e. become w, y) in all the other languages. In
Somali intervocalic w regularly continues *ww, whereas intervocalic *w became b, as noted
earlier. Final w continues both *w and *ww. The rule $w \to b/V\underline{\quad}V$ must have operated in
Somali after the loss of final gemination, because final w becomes b once vowel initial
suffixes are attached, regardless of whether it derives from *w or from *ww. Thus *kaww-
→ kow 'one', but koob-iyo-toban 'eleven' (*aw-V → oob-V, except after ħ, ᶜ, q, ᵓ, h → ab-V,
cf. ħabaal).

Examples:

*ħawwaal- 'grave'; to bury' (cf. *ħawaal-[18]): Som. ħawaal-; Galla awwaal-; Gidole awwaal-
probably < Galla.

*kaww- 'alone': Somali, Rendille, and Boni kow 'one'; Konso xaww-aa 'alone, separate,
different', Gidole haww 'id.'. Galla m. ko·eesa, f. ko·eettii 'alone', ko·om- 'become
lonely', caus. koɬ-siis- 'make lonely' reflect *kaw-.

*ᵓayyaan- 'spirit, good luck' (→ 'feast'): Som. ayaan; Galla ayyaan-a, Konso ayyaan-a,
Gidole ayyaan; Sid. ayaan-a (probably misheard for ayyaan-a), Had. ayyaan-o; Burji ayyaan-a;
Gollango and Dobase ayyaan-a.

*guyy- 'day': Galla guyy-aa, Konso kuyy-aata; Gawwada kuyy-anko, Gollango kuyy-u 'today'.

*ᵓaayy- 'mother': Som. aay-o 'stepmother', Rend. ay-o, Boni aay-o', Baiso ay-o; Galla
aayy-oo, Konso aayy-o; Had. ayy-a 'sister' (the original meaning is still apparent in
ay-minee 'mater familias'; Burji aayy-ee, and probably also Saho-Afar aay-a 'older brother
or sister'. A reduplicated form *yaayy- comparable to Dasenech baaba, Gawwada papp-o
(both < PEC *baabb-) 'father' is probably the basis of Afar yay-a 'mama' and Dullay yaayy-e
'mother'.

The sequences "short vowel + w or y + consonant or word boundary" (i.e. y or w in closed
syllables) tend to form diphthongs and have therefore undergone special developments in
several daughter languages.

---

[17]This hypothesis would neatly account for quite a number of otherwise problematic PEC
variants. For instance, there is as yet no systematic way to correlate a variety of
similar but distinct forms with the meaning 'horn': Saho-Afar gays-a, Som. gees,
elsewhere *gaas-. By assuming a pre-PEC form *gaawis- → *gaais- = *gaays-, the Saho-
Afar form would be a regularly shortened version of *gaays-a. Somali gees would be
derivable from *gaais- by an independently motivated rule (umlaut of *aa before *i). In
all EC languages other than Saho-Afar, i may be assumed to disappear between aa and C.

[18]A third stem *ħawl- is underlying Konso hawl- 'bury' and Gollango ħawl-e 'grave'.

*-aw- and *-ay- were certainly the most frequent of these combinations in PEC, and their reconstruction is well supported in numerous cases.  They will be discussed in full below. Let us first try to present some evidence for other less solidly supported combinations.

It can be assumed that PEC had at least *ey, *oy, *iy in preconsonantal position across a morpheme boundary; on the assumption that suffixes beginning in a consonant were regularly attached to nominal stems, the existence of *uy+C must also be presumed.

There is no evidence for morpheme-internal sequences of VyC other than ayC, and no evidence for sequences of VwC other than awC, regardless of whether morpheme-internal or not.

*eyC/*oyC is attested in verbal forms such as *dey-taa/*doy-taa, 2s of *dey-/*doy- 'look at'. As can be seen from the individual reflexes of such forms, *ey must have merged with *ay in all languages in which it can be traced and consequently shows the individual reflexes of *ay which are discussed below.  There is no indication of the fate of *oyC sequences in Somali and other Omo-Tana languages except for the verb *goy- 'cut' (Rend. goy-, Boni koy-), which seems to retain its y in word-final and preconsonantal position.  In Somali, however, this verb is irregular, and displays the stem allomorphs goo- and goʔ-.  oyC is generally retained as such in Konso and Gidole.  No trace of a sequence with short o before y was found in Galla, but cf. boo-sa, boo-nya (Bor. boo-nna), 2s and 1p respectively of booy- 'weep'.  A similar treatment can also be presumed for other possible oyC sequences.

The only relevant case for *uy is *kuy- 'anthill', already referred to above.  Since this continues as Galla kuy-sa, Konso kuy-ta, Gidole huy-t (i.e. kuy- + singulative suffix -t-), it can be concluded that the sequence *uyC remained unchanged at least in Macro-Oromo.

Saho-Afar, Burji, and Dullay have several words with oyC and uyC sequences, some of which may continue such sequences from PEC, and only on this assumption can it be hypotesized that these languages retained such sequences in unchanged form.  I was not able to find any relevant cognate sets, however.

The only example for an iy sequence is provided by *biy- 'earth' (cf. Dullay piy-e, Hadiyya bey-o 'place'; Galla biyy-a and biyy-ee with secondary gemination).  This yields bii in preconsonantal position and before word-boundary, e.g. in Galla bii-ti (subject case of biyy-a), Konso pii-ta (singulative), Arbore and Dasenech bii, and Elmolo biˑʔ.

PEC *ayC and *awC regularly continue as such only in Saho-Afar, Konso-Gidole, HEC, Burji (where ay alternates with ey), and Dullay.

In Somali *ayC and *awC have split into ayC, eyC, eeC, and awC, owC, respectively.  The monophthongization eeC for *ayC is found only in a handful of cases where C is y, e.g. gay-y → geey- 'bring', *yeyy- → *yayy- → yeey 'wolf'.  The distribution of the remaining variants is quite regular:  a is preserved after h, q, ʕ, ħ and initially (i.e. after *ʔ), otherwise it becomes e before y, o before w.

In Rendille and apparently also in Baiso ay and aw are monophthongized into e(e) and o(o) respectively in preconsonantal position.  For Boni and Dasenech the individual reflexes of *ay and *aw in preconsonantal position are not easy to determine.  In two cases *aw became Boni aa: *gaws- 'molar' → kaas, and *ʕawš-'grass' → aasᵉʔ.  In one case, however, it appears as uu (*gawraʕ- 'cut throat', Som. gowraʕ-, Boni kuuraʔ- 'butcher') and in another case as oo (*ʔawr- → oor 'bull elephant').  ii seems to be the regular Boni reflex of *ay whenever Somali has ey: Som. feyd- 'undress' = Boni fiid- 'uncover', Som. weyn 'big' = Boni wiin.  Evidence for Dasenech is scanty; ʔiiš 'grass' can be assumed to derive from *ʕayš- (via ʔeyš; *ʕa regularly →, ʔe); *ʔaw is retained in ʔawr-ic 'he-camel'.

In Galla, *ay before a consonant regularly continues as ee.  The reflexes of *aw are quite chaotic.  It appears as *oo* in *ooꞩ-oo* 'burden camels' < *ᵓawꞩ-, but as *oꞩ* in a similar environment in *goꞩꞩa*(ᵓ)- = Som. *gowꞩa*ᶜ- (PEC *gawꞩa*ᶜ- 'slaughter'), and *w* is metathesized in *d'oꞩw-* = *d'o*(*w*)*aꞩ-* 'prohibit, prevent, defend' = Som. *ɖawꞩ-* 'protect', Konso and Gid. *d'awꞩ-* 'forbid', Burji *d'ooꞩ-* 'forbid' (PEC *d'awꞩ-* 'prevent').  An utterly amazing reflex of preconsonantal *aw* is found in the preconsonantal allomorph of the denominative suffix: -*aw-a* : -*oꞩ-ta* (the same reflex occurs in *koꞩ-siis-* < *kaw-siis-* 'make lonely').

Examples of PEC *ay* and *aw* in closed syllables:

*ᵓ*ay-, preconsonantal and pausal variant of PEC *ᵓ*ayy- 'who, which': Saho *ay* 'who'; Boni *ai* 'who'; Galla *ee-nnu* 'who', *ee-sa* 'where', Konso and Gidole *ay-nu* 'who', Konso *ay-ša* 'where'; Sidamo *ay*, Hadiyya *ay*.  (The prevocalic allomorph *ᵓ*ayy- is reflected in Somali *ay-o* 'who', Sid. *ayy-e* 'who', Hadiyya *ayy-ím* 'whoever').

*ᶜ*awl- 'brown, yellow': Saho ᶜ*owl-a* 'dust storm'; Somali ᶜ*awl-* 'yellow'; Konso *awl-* 'brown'; Dullay ᶜ*awl-* 'yellow'.

*ᵓ*awꞩ- 'large male animal': Saho *awꞩ* 'bull'; Som. *awꞩ* 'he-camel', Rend. *oꞩ* 'he-camel, bull', Boni *ooꞩ* 'male elephant', Das. ᵓ*awꞩ-ic* 'he camel'; Galla *ooꞩ-oo* 'burden camels'.

*-*ay-t-* singulative suffix : Saho -*ayt-*, Galla -*ees-*, Konso and Gidole -*ayt-*, Burji -*eyš-*.

*-*aw-* denominative suffix, *-*ayš-* causative of denominative suffix: Saho -*aw-*, -*ays-*; Somali -*ow-*, -*eey-*, Boni -*ow-*, -*e*(*í*)/*ee*, Das. -*a*(*b*)-, -*ay/c-*; Galla -*aw-*, -*ees-*, Konso -*aw-*, -*ayš-*, Gidole -*aw-*, -*ayy-*; Burji -*aw-*, -*eyš-*; Dullay -*aw-*, -*as-* (cf. below).

*ħayd'- 'fat': Som. *ħayɖ*, Konso *hayd'-a*, Gid. *hayd'-a*, Dullay *hayd'-o*.

In concluding this chapter, let us discuss the evidence for a PEC morphophonemic rule deleting semivowels in the position V___CC.  In Konso and Gidole the paradigms of the *ayš- causative are as follows:

|      | Konso     | Gidole    |
|------|-----------|-----------|
| 1s   | -ayš-a    | -ayy-a    |
| 2s   | -as -sa   | -at -ta   |
| 3sm  | -ayš-a    | -ayy-a    |
| 3sf  | -as -sa   | -at -ta   |
| 1p   | -an -na   | -an -na   |
| 2p   | -as -san  | -at -tane |
| 3p   | -ayš-an   | -ayy-ane  |

These forms are regularly derived from *-*ayš-a*, *-*ayš-ta*, *-*ayš-na* etc. by a rule which operated in Proto-Konsoid and had the following form:

$$y \rightarrow \emptyset \ / \ V \ \underline{\phantom{xx}} \ C{+}C$$

Underlying */ayš+ta/ and */ayš+na/ had previously become *ays-ta* and *ays-na* by the rule *š → s/* ___ C mentioned in 4.16.  Then the rule of *y*-deletion changed these sequences into *as-ta* and *as-na*, which finally became Konso *assa*, *anna* and Gidole *atta*, *anna* by assimilation.

This phenomenon is by no means isolated.  There is a good deal of variation between $V{w \brace y}C$

and VC sequences in some varieties of Saho (notably that described by Reinisch 1889) which suggests that a similar but even more general rule of semivowel deletion may have been operating in an earlier stage of Saho-Afar.

There are good reasons to believe that a general rule of semivowel deletion before consonant clusters was already part of the morphophonemic structure of PEC, because relics of this rule can be found in nearly every EC language.  Dullay was clearly one of the last languages to abandon it, since it was still operating when the typical Dullay suffixes m. -*ko*, f. *te* were attached to the PEC roots.  *\**ᶜ*awš-ko* thus became *ᶜaš-ko* 'grass', the singulative ending -*ayt*- + -*ko* became -*at-ko* (and subsequently *akko* by assimilation), cf. \**gelz-ayt*- (Galla *jald-ees*-, Konso and Gidole *kelt-ayt*-) + -*ko* becomes Dullay *kals-akko*. The preconsonantal causative allomorph -*as*- was, however, generalized; the alternation \*-*ayš*- ~ \*-*as*- is no longer operative.  Some cases of dialectal variation within Dullay are also instructive, e.g. Dobase *lawl-e* 'clothing' vs. Gollango and Gawwada *lall-e*.  The latter form regularly derives from \**lal-l-e*.

The following is an example of how this rule could explain a variety of otherwise problematic correspondences.  Compare the following cognate set:

Saho *awaᶜ* 'approaching thunderstorm'; Somali *qaw*, *qaᶜ* 'different kinds of noises', Konso *qaww-a* 'different kinds of noises', Gidole *k'ak'aww-a* 'lightning', Gawwada *qawwaᶜ-akko* 'thunder', Harso *qawwaᶜ-ko* 'thunder'.

All these forms could easily be subsumed under a reconstruction \**k'awᶜ*-.  A root such as this would regularly split into three allomorphs:  a prevocalic \**k'aw*- (provided that no restructuring of postconsonantal ᶜ took place), a preconsonantal \**k'aᶜ*-, and a "distributive" or "plural" form \**k'awwaᶜ*-.  The distrubutive variant survives in the Saho and Dullay forms.  In Somali, both \**k'aᶜ*- and \**k'aw*- were retained; Burji generalized the preconsonantal variant with loss of *w*.  The Konso-Gidole forms are ambiguous; they may either derive from \**k'awᶜ*- directly (i.e. from a base with restructured preconsonantal \*ᶜ) or from \**k'aw*-, in which case the *ww* would be secondary (plural or Dullay influence).

## 4.20.  PEC \**k'*

The ancestor of the consonant traditionally transcribed as *q*, *ḳ*, *k'*, *K* and so on in the individual languages, is set up here as a glottalized voiceless velar stop \**k'*.  A possible alternative would be the reconstruction of an uvular *q*; it was felt, however, that a glottalized proto-phoneme would better account for some of the observed sound changes. First of all, in Galla, HEC, Burji, part of the Konso-Gidole group including Gidole itself, and in some varieties of Dullay, we actually find the pronunciation *k'*.  Secondly, in a number of languages such as Saho-Afar, Sidamo, Elmolo, Boni, and Dasenech, some or all of its occurrences have become ʾ or subsequently zero.  Reduction to glottal stop is a tendency normally found with glottalized consonants, but less common with uvulars.  Dasenech and Elmolo have *g'*, a voiced velar implosive stop, and such a sound is universally considered to be the voiced counterpart of *k'*.  Only in Somali, Konso, some varieties of Dullay, and possibly Rendille do we find uvular articulation without glottalization.  Since the majority of the EC languages thus point in the direction of glottalization, we consider this feature original.  From a phonetic point of view it seems more plausible to assume the two articulation gestures involved in producing the complex sound *k'* (velar and glottal) to have met somewhere in the middle (at the uvular point) than to assume a "split" of an uvular articulation into a velar and a glottal one.

PEC \**k'* has the following reflexes: Somali *q* (uvular plosive with voiced, voiceless, and fricative allophones), palatalized into *j* before *e* and *i*, Rendille *x*, Boni ʾ (initially zero), Baiso zero, Dasenech *g'* initially, ʾ finally and zero medially, Elmolo zero (probably ʾ) initially, *g'* or zero medially depending on the environment, Galla *k'*, palatalized into *c'* before *e* and *i*, Gidole *k'*, Konso *q* (voiced uvular plosive; voiceless when doubled), Burji *k'*, Dullay *q* or *k'* depending on the dialect, and Yaaku *q*.

The reflexes of *\*k'* in Saho-Afar and in HEC are somewhat problematic. Whereas the usual reflex of *\*k'* in both groups appears to be, ˀ or zero, one can find a number of words with irregular preservation of *\*k'* (which, in the case of Saho-Afar, shifted to *k*).

Let us first examine the Saho-Afar case, which may possibly be more easily handled than the HEC problem. Hayward (1974) has convincingly demonstrated that there is no *q* (whether glottalized or uvular) in Afar, and that the few occurrences of *q* in Saho are either confined to loanwords or secondarily derived from *\*k*. In any case, the reflexes of PEC *\*k'* are either zero or *k*. The zero reflex is by far the more frequent. Some examples are given below.

Loss of *\*k'*:

*uʃuᶜ-* 'cough' < PEC *\*k'uʃᶜ-*, cf. 4.8.

*-usul-* 'laugh' (pref.) < PEC *\*k'sol-/\*k'osl-*, cf. 4.14.

*or-* 'hew' < *\*k'or-* 'wood' (Som. *qor-i*, Das. *g'or*, Elm. *or-o'*, Galla *k'or-aani*, Konso *qoyr-a*, Gid. *k'oyr-* etc.).

*awaᶜ* 'approaching thunderstorm' < PEC *\*k'awᶜ-*, cf. 4.19.

*all-o* 'vanity' < PEC *\*k'all-*, cf. 4.11. There is also a prefix verb Afar *-elell-* 'become beaten, loose' which belongs to the same root.

*aɖ-* 'cut the hair' (Reinisch) < *\*k'aɖ'₁-*, cf. 4.15.

*arar* 'mountain top' < PEC *\*k'ar-* 'point, peak-top' (Som. *qar* 'hill higher than *kur*', Galla *k'ar-r-ee* 'peak' etc.).

*ʃi(y)-* 'sweep' < PEC *\*ʃiik'-*, cf. below.

*bool* 'hundred' < PEC *\*bok'l-*, cf. Som. *boqol*.

*\*k'* → *k*:

*kab-* 'seize' < PEC *\*k'ab-* 'take, have', cf. 4.4.

*koroʃ-o* 'bark' < PEC *\*k'olʃ-* 'id.' (Som. *qoloʃ*, Galla *k'oloʃ-a* 'foreskin', Konso *qolʃ-a*).

*bak-* 'crush' < PEC *\*bak'-* (Som. *baq-* 'curdle', Galla *bak'-* 'melt', *bak'ak'-* 'crack' etc.).

*ḥokuk-* 'scratch' < PEC *\*ḥok'-*, cf. below.

*-ootok-* 'strike' < PEC *\*-tak'-/-tuk'-*, a former prefix verb which continues as suffixing in Rendille *tax-*, Das. *ṭaˀ-* 'push'; Galla *tuk'-* 'touch'.

It is noteworthy that these five words with a *k* reflex of *k'* are the only attestations of this sound change in Saho-Afar that I have found so far, whereas the examples for a zero reflex could easily be doubled. This suggests that the reflex of *\*k'* in Saho-Afar is basically zero, and that the *k* reflex is exceptional.

Since in three of these five cases *\*k'* is the final consonant of a verbal root, it can perhaps be assumed that these verbs derive from earlier singularitives with final gemination.  The singularitive is used with *bak'- in Gidole and Dullay (pakk'- and paqq-, respectively).  This would explain the occurrence of k from *kk'.  kab- 'seize' and koroɓ-o 'bark' cannot, however, be explained in this way.

In HEC, *k' is generally retained as such after consonants, and as a geminate kk'.  For the former cf. Sid. bank'-o, Had. baank'-o 'lightning' (PEC *bark'-/*birk'-, cf. Dasenech bidd'i < *birk'-ti, Elmolo i-birg'-a etc.), for the latter cf. Had. bukk'-am- melt', a singularitive of the root *bak'-/*buk'- mentioned earlier.

In both Sidamo and Hadiyya many words with initial k' have been recorded, but only a few of these have any bearing on the reconstruction of PEC *k'.  Yet there are at least three common HEC words with initial k': *k'ub- 'finger' (Sid. k'ubb-e, Had. k'ub-aᵓa), *k'iiz- 'cold' (Sid., Dar., Had. k'iid-, Al. k'iiz-), and Sidamo k'as-, Had. k'aass- 'stab'.  Moreover, Hadiyya k'aar-a 'sharpness' is cognate with Konso qaar-ta, Gid. k'ar-a 'id.'; the root is *k'ar- 'sharp', probably related to *k'ar- 'peak'.

On the other hand, there are quite a number of solidly supported instances of a zero reflex of *k'- in HEC:

*k'udħ- 'thorn': Sid. uta, Had. utta,

*k'osl- 'laugh': Sid., Dar., Al. osol-, Had. osaar-,

*k'al- 'slaughter': Had. alaleess-,

*k'eb- 'break': Had. app'- 'separate',

and several others.

In medial position the situation is similar.  Zero (or ᵓ) reflexes can be found in, e.g. Had., Sid. ɓi(ᵓ)- 'sweep' < *ɓiik'-, Sid. daᵓ- 'come', Had. t'aᵓ- 'go' < *dak'-, Had. waqᵓ-a 'god' < *waak'-, Had. loom-ee 'Adam's apple' < *luk'm-.  On the other hand, Darasa has ɓik'- 'sweep', and there is also a common HEC *mik'- 'bone' (cf. Dullay miq-), and Hadiyya lik'-ic'- (PEC *lik'-/*luk'-) 'swallow'.  In view of this jungle of irregularities, it is difficult to conceive of any plausible solution.

Before presenting a number of cognate sets to exemplify the reflexes of PEC *k' in the individual languages, a word on Arbore may be in order.  Being as yet one of the most poorly attested EC languages, the available Arbore data can be quoted only with extreme caution.  As far as the reflexes of *k' are concerned, the transcription found in the various sources appears to be highly unreliable.  In Linton et al. both k and k' appear as a reflex of *k', and the phonetic correlate of this grapheme is unknown (e.g. kor-o 'tree' for PEC *k'or-, k'uyiyᵓoa 'wet' for PEC *k'oyy-, and there is also a ᵓ reflex in waqᵓ-a 'god' < PEC *waak'-).  Since k' also appears where g is expected (cf. ak'eš- 'kill' = Galla ajees-), it seems wise not to trust the transcription too much in this point.

Examples of initial *k':

*k'ab- 'cold': Som. qab-ow, Rendille xob-ob (noun), xob- (adj.), Baiso a-m-b-ali (with secondary nasalization), Arbore keb-eta, Elmolo -ap-an-; Galla k'ab-an-, Konso qap-p-ann-aaw- 'become cool (liquids)', Gidole k'ap-p-an-aw- 'become cool', k'ap-p-an-ot 'coolness'.

*k'eb- 'become broken': Somali jab-, Rendille jeb-, Dasenech g'e(b)-; Galla c'ab-, Konso qep-; Hadiyya app'- 'part'.

*k'udħ- 'thorn': Somali qodaħ, Rendille kudaħ (?), Elmolo ed' (from a variant *k'adħ-); Galla k'oraa-ttii; Sid. ut-a, Had. utt-a (d → t by assimilation to h which later disappears).

Cf. also Gidole *k'udd'-eet*, Konso *qeet-ta* with problematic correspondences.

Examples of medial *\*k'*:

*\*ɓiik'-* 'sweep' Saho-Afar *ɓi-*; Somali *ɓiiq-*, Das. *ɓiiy-a*, imp. *ɓiiʔ* 'wipe'; Sidamo *ɓi-*, Hadiyya *ɓiiʔ-*, Darasa *ɓik'-*.

*\*ħek'-/\*ħok'-* 'scratch': Saho *ħokuk-*; Som. *ħoq-*, *ħaqħaq-*, Rend. *ox-*, Boni *hoʔ-*, Arb. *hek-* Galla *hook'-*, Gid. *hek'-*; Burji *hok'ook'-*.

PEC *\*kk'* is attested in at least two solidly supported reconstructions: *\*dikk'-/dukk'-* 'small': Som. *diiq-* 'become faint, tenuous', *diiq* 'faintness', Galla *dikk'-a* 'small', Hadiyya *t'ukk'-a* 'narrow' (*d → t'* by assimilation to *k'*), and Harso *tiikk'-assa* 'small'. Cf. also *\*d'₁ookk'-* 'mud', 4.15.


## 4.21.  PEC *\*ʔ*

Medial *\*ʔ* is firmly established on the basis of correspondences such as 'meat', Somali *soʔ*, Galla *ɓoo-ni*, Gidole *soʔ-a* (dial. *soh-a*), Bussa *spʔ-o*, Dasenech *so*, all of them going back to PEC *\*soʔ-*; or Somali *baʔ-*, Sidamo *baʔ-*, Hadiyya *biʔ-* 'become obliterated, destroyed' PEC *\*baʔ-*. We assume, then, that PEC had a full-fledged phoneme *\*ʔ* whose distribution may have been approximately that of other consonant phonemes, i.e. which occurred in initial as well as in medial position. However, whereas the reconstruction of medial *\*ʔ* is un-problematic (except for the fact that only a few languages provide evidence for *\*ʔ* because of the frequent merger of *ʔ* and *ᶜ*), the reconstruction of *ʔ* in initial position of-fers serious methodological difficulties. In nearly all EC languages, *ʔ* is optional before initial vowels and is therefore counted as a junction marker rather than the manifestation an underlying phoneme /ʔ/ in word-initial position. For Somali, Armstrong (1934) states: "It appears to be nearly always possible to use *ʔ* before a vowel in an initial syllable and it need not therefore be represented in this position." Exactly the same statement could be made for Galla, but in his phonological description of Borana Galla, Andrzejewski does not even mention this fact. His phoneme *ʔ* does not occur initially. The description of Welmers (on Saho) and Mahaffy (on Afar) indicate that initial vowels are generally preceded by a glottal stop. This is also true of HEC, Burji, and Dullay, but none of the authors who deal with all these languages have ever treated initial glottal stops as phonemic. This is in accordance with traditional phonological theory which prescribes that predictable phenomena should be regarded as redundant. Hence, for example, German *ʔ* is not counted as a phoneme, because its occurrence is entirely predictable. It is found only in positions where it can be inserted by a general automatic rule. In the case of most of the EC languages, the situation is entirely different. Since *ʔ* occurs in position other than initial, its occurrence is predictable only in one specific position viz., initially. But such an interpretation could arbitrarily be conceived for any phoneme in any language of the world. A careful examination of the relevant facts indicates that only advantages can be gained from the interpretation of initial *ʔ* as phonemic. Because of the rigid restrictions on word and syllable structure, there are only a few shapes in which EC words can appear. The number of these shapes would be doubled (and, accordingly, the statement of the shapes unnecessarily complicated), if shapes with initial vowel were permitted. A good case can therefore be made "for structural reasons" for reconstructing *ʔ* in initial position. Moreover, since there are many minimal pairs such as Somali *ag* 'nearness' vs. *ᶜag* 'foot' in most of the individual languages, the "structural zero" before the initial vowels has always been regarded as a meaningful absence of something which contrasts with initial C. Now as there is no zero, but a concrete occurrence of *ʔ*, it is of course this *ʔ* that contrasts with other initial consonants. And finally, since it is possible to assign this *ʔ* to a phoneme already posited for medial position but not occurring initially, it would indeed be foolish not to do so.

Aside from these abstract considerations, evidence can be presented for the interpretation of initial ꜣ as underlying /ꜣ/ in various languages. In Galla, a reduplicated initial vowel occurs as, ꜣV medially, as in *iꜣilᵃ*, plural of *ilᵃ* 'eye'. This is a quite general process in Galla: wherever initial vowels slip into medial position, ꜣ shows up. Since this, ꜣ is as unstable as initial, ꜣ, it could be interpreted as an optional element resolving vowel clusters, were it not for the fact that there are vowel clusters that never insert, ꜣ (e.g. for *d'o·ar-* 'prevent' my informants categorically reject the pronunciation *d'oꜣar-*). Reduplication can likewise be used for evidencing initial /ꜣ/ in Konso and Gidole, cf. Gidole *alꜣalt* 'protuberance on neck of goat' (a reduplicated stem ꜣ*al-*), or Konso *iꜣꜣik-* 'intensive stem of *ik-* 'drink', which is formed according to the familiar pattern of intensive formation, cf. *d'add'am-* from *d'am-* 'eat'. Were 'drink' to be interpreted as underlying /ik/ rather than /ꜣik/, there would be no morphophonemic motivation of double, ꜣ in *iꜣꜣik-*. In these two examples Konso and Gidole /ꜣ/ derive historically from PEC *ꜥ rather than from *ꜣ, but the intensive pattern of the type *iꜣꜣik-* is by no means restricted to ꜣ's that derive from *ꜥ, cf. *o ꜣꜣool-* from *ool-* 'spend the day' (PEC *ꜣ*ool-* 'stay').

There are still stronger indications that initial /ꜣ/ plays a distinctive role in the sound pattern of Konso and Gidole. Both languages make extensive use of selectors (i.e. preverbal morphemes indicating person and aspect/tense). In Gidole the first person selectors end in a nasal whose point of articulation features are assimilated to a following consonant (i.e. the initial consonant of the verb stem): *m* before labials, *n* before dentals, *ny* before palatals, ŋ before velars etc. ŋ also occurs before vowels and *h*. Presumably it was this curiosity that led Black (1974) to the assumption that the underlying representation of the first person selector ends in ŋ (normally, the position before vowels is the most neutral position for nasals, i.e. the one least affected by morphophonemic distortions). However, such an interpretation would create a unique situation here: the first person selector *heŋ* would be the only Gidole morpheme with an underlying ŋ phoneme. From a morphophonemic point of view this is totally undesirable, but also totally unnecessary, because if V- were regarded as ꜣV- (that's how it actually sounds), a significant generalization concerning nasal assimilation could be stated (e.g. *n* → ŋ before all back non-vocalic segments), and the problem would be solved in a natural way. Konso has no such assimilation of *n* before glottals. Here it is the second person selector which clearly demonstrates the presence of underlying /ꜣ/ before initial vowels. Characteristic of this morpheme is the fact that it ends in an archi-consonant which is totally assimilated to all following consonants. Black sets up underlying ꜣ to represent this archi-consonant, and he was undoubtedly induced to do this by the fact that it shows up as, ꜣ before vowels. However, in the pronunciation of our mutual informant Shako Otto, this, ꜣ was generally long: *iꜣ ꜣik-ta* 'you are drinking' (Black would transcribe *iꜣ ikta*). The only way I see to account for this fact is the assumption that verb stems with initial vowel really begin with ꜣ and that the ꜣ of the selector is a total assimilation of the archi-consonant as in all the other cases (cf. *id' d'am-ta* 'you are eating', *ih has-ta* 'you are staying' etc.).

The same mechanism is operative in the Dullay languages, and the interpretation just proposed for Konso is also the only plausible solution here: *ax xaɓ-ti* 'you came', *ap pat-ti* 'you disappeared', and, accordingly, *aꜣ ꜣerak-ti* 'you sent'.

In Dasenech there are no initial vowels at all, neither in the phonological representation, nor in the phonetic output. In this language initial, ꜣ (which is never optional) contrasts with a slightly aspirated vocalic onset, approximately *ȟ*, represented as *h* in this paper. Both of them pattern as consonants and constitute a phonological class together with the velars. Heine's (1973) description of Elmolo indicates a situation similar to that in Dasenech with the further peculiarity that *n* becomes ŋ before ꜣ as in Gidole.

These considerations lead to the assumption that initial ꜣ has a phonemic status in at least most of the EC languages. We further assume that this is a trace of the PEC sound pattern and consequently reconstruct the proto-forms of vowel-initial roots with ꜣ, e.g. *ꜣ*aɓ- 'mouth', as represented by Somali *aɓ*, Galla *aɓ-aani*, Das. ꜣ*aɓ-u* etc.

Let us now return to the problem of medial *ᵓ.  Paul Black (1974) finds only three examples of PLEC *ᵓ, all of them being in postvocalic and root-final position.

*lo ᵓ- 'cows' (coll.):  Afar lo-w (perhaps phonemically lo-o), and with progressive assimilation, la-a; Somali loᵓ; Galla loo-ni, Konso low-aa < lo-aa, Gidole loh-a; Dullay loᵓ-o 'cow'.  Dasenech lo- as a prefix in ox-names also belongs here.

*maᵓ 'negative particle': Afar ma, Som. maᵓ, Das. ma etc.

*leᵓ- 'die' (plural subject): Som. leᵓ-, Konso le(y)-, Sidamo reᵓ-, Hadiyya leh- etc.

To these may be added *soᵓ- 'meat' and *baᵓ- 'be destroyed' cited above.  Black reconstructs the word for 'meat' as *soᶜ-, obviously overlooking the Somali equivalent soᵓ, and the Dasenech evidence which also indicates the reconstruction of a glottal stop rather than a pharyngeal:  whereas word-final *ᶜ continues as Das. ᵓ (cf. 4.17), a glottal stop is represented by zero, and the word for 'meat' is so[19] with a zero second radical.

From these comparisons it is evident that PEC medial *ᵓ continues as Saho-Afar Ø, Somali ᵓ, and Dullay ᵓ, and that it has merged with ᶜ to yield ᵓ, h, y, w, Ø or length according to language and environment in the Macro-Oromo group (cf. 4.17).  The items for 'die' and 'be destroyed' suggest reflexes very similar to those of Macro-Oromo in HEC.

A certain amount of new evidence for ᵓ emerges from the Omo-Tana data recently collected by Heine (Rendille and Boni).

Boni saᵓan 'foot(print)' and the related Galla faan-a 'footprint, heel etc.' may go back either to *saᶜn- or to *saᵓn-.  The Dasenech equivalent saan-a indicates however, a proto-form with a glottal stop PEC *saᵓn-, because if a pharyngeal were present in the proto-form, Dasenech should have e instead of a (cf. 4.17).  From this example, as well as from comparisons such as Som. daᵓ- = Boni taᵓ- 'rain', it can be concluded that PEC *ᵓ continues as such in Boni, at least in intervocalic position.  An indication for PEC *ᵓ can also be found in Boni saᵓ 'time', saᵓaa' 'morning', Rendille sah 'late morning', Galla faa-taa 'morning coffee; good morning!', and perhaps Dullay saᵓ-a 'recently'.  This cognate set, for which PEC *saᵓ- may be posited, suggests a zero reflex of *ᵓ in intervocalic position in Somali, and an h reflex of *ᵓ in Rendille.  These correspondences are also apparent in the following cognate set:

PEC *naᵓs- 'woman's breast': Som. naas, Baiso naas-i, Rendille nahas, Boni naᵓas.

As in the case of *saᵓn- 'footprint' above, each attestation contributes in some way to the disambiguation of the others.  The Somali and Baiso forms taken together would lead to the reconstruction *naas-.  This is contradicted by the Rendille and Boni forms which clearly demonstrate the presence of some medial consonant.  Both Rendille h and Boni ᵓ are, however, ambiguous; they might indicate a glottal or a pharyngeal.  h is ruled out by Boni ᵓ, but Rendille h = Boni ᵓ could be subsumed under PEC *ᶜ.  Pharyngeal loss in Somali, though scarcely tolerable because of the long aa, would be a possible explanation, were it not for the Baiso form which clearly demonstrates the absence of any pharyngeal in the proto-form because of its a which would have to be e if the proto-form were *naᶜs-.

There are two cognate sets which show a zero reflex of *ᵓ in Somali, albeit in final position.

---

[19]This word was erroneously cited as su in some of my earlier publications.

*ri²- 'goat': Somali ri, pl. ri-yo, Rendille rih-i, pl. ri-yo; Galla re²-ee (vowel assimilation across, ²).

*gu²- 'rainy season, year': Somali gu, pl. gu-yo, Rendille guh, pl. guh-ah.

The word for 'goat' is actually attested as ri² for Southern Somali.  In the absence of any evidence to the contrary it may be hypothesized that the loss of the ² was caused by some following consonant (presumably that of the plural ending -yo) and then generalized. In a case such as lo²-yo (plural of lo² 'cowherd') the opposite process must then be assumed.

A zero reflex of, ² in preconsonantal position can also be posited for Rendille, cf. the plural of rih-i 'goat', ri-yo; also loil-yo 'cattle', and da-to 'rain', from *lo²- and *da²-, respectively.

It is possible that many occurrences of PEC *² in medial position to consonants are "hidden" in the form of irregular correspondences of the type described by Black (1974:210):  The correspondence among Afar biak 'illness', Som. buk(-ood)- 'become ill', and Konso paaq- 'become ill' could perhaps be accounted for by means of a reconstruction of the shape *bV²k-; the cluster *²k would be taken to yield Konso q and Somali k.  Similarly the correspondence among Somali siib-, sibq- 'slip, be slippery', and similar meanings, Rendille sub 'mud', Galla sup'-ee 'clay', and Gollango sip-te 'loam' could be subsumed under a reconstruction *sib²-/*sub²-.  We have already noted that Galla p' seems to continue the clusters ²b and b² in at least two relatively certain cases (nyaap'-a 'enemy', where p' is from ᶜb via ²b, and upp'-e 'I knew', an irregular 1s perfect form of the verb hub-ad't-, which derives from *hub-²ee[20]).  A similar case is the irregular correspondence between Somali laab and Galla lap'-ee 'breastbone', which, under the assumption of "hidden" ²'s would turn out to be regular reflexes of PEC *la²b- (Somali) or *lab²- (Galla).

---

[20]According to the "Praetorius hypothesis" the Cushitic aspect/tense suffixes derive from an earlier prefix verb 'to be', the first person singular of which must have had an initial ².

## APPENDIX A

### Notes on the historical phonology of Yaaku

Both phonologically and gramatically, Yaaku is by far the most deviant of all EC languages. In the following, only the most conspicuous changes will be summarized as a guide to the future analysis of the historical phonology of Yaaku.

*a → e in the neighborhood of pharyngeals: *d'amħ- 'cold' → dɛhm-o; *k'uɓaᶜ- 'cough' → qopɛʔɛ- etc.

Roots of the form CaCC- appear as CiCa(C)-: *matħ- 'head' → mitɛh, *zagm- 'honey' → sikaʔ, *ganᶜ- 'palm of hand' → kinneʔ.

*b, *d, *g become p, t, k: *beel- 'get lost' → peel-, *dub- 'bake' → tuup- 'cook', *seg- 'far' → sɛkɛʔ-.

*k and *g are sometimes palatalized to ç and j, respectively: *kebᶜ- 'leopard' → çɛʔp-e', *magin- 'foot, leg' (Som. majin, Galla manj-ii) → miji.

*k' continues as q, but there are several instances of palatalization of *k' into j: *k'ub- 'finger' → qop-e, *k'uɓaᶜ- 'cough' → qopɛʔɛ-; *murk'- 'gristle' (Som. muruq 'muscle', Konso murq-a 'soft bud', Gidole mork'-a 'bone of nose, soft part of ensete') → morj-i'.

On the reflexes of *d' and *d'₁ cf. 4.15.

*ɓ becomes p (cf. 4.8): *kuɓ- 'fall' → kup- 'die', *kesɓ- 'chest' → kɛhp-en.

Both *s and *š normally continue as s: *seg- 'far' → sɛkɛʔ, *warš- 'rhino' → orsɛ-. Final and preconsonantal s become h; this is in accordance with still productive morphophonemic rules: *ʔis- 'self' → eh, *d'ib-iš-a 'he covers' → dep-ih.

*ħ and *ᶜ continue as h and ʔ, respectively: *hadd'- 'bitter' (Ga.Ko.Gi. hadd'- , Boni hareer, Rend. hadad) → hɛid-oo, *matħ- 'head' → mitɛh; *kaᶜ- 'get up' → kɛʔ-. Neither consonant occurs as second member of a consonant cluster and both are metathesized if they occur in such clusters in the morphophonemic structure: mitɛh 'head', pl. miht-en, kinneʔ 'palm of hand', pl. kiʔn-ɛi.

Loss of final consonants is common: *zagm- → sikaʔ (pl. sakm-ai), *magin- → miji (pl. mijn-ɛn), *ᶜarrab- 'tongue' → ɛrɛ (pl. ɛrɛp-a').

APPENDIX B

Summary of reflexes of PEC obstruents

The reflexes of PEC obstruents that have been discussed in 4 will be summarized here in tabular form for the best attested languages Saho-Afar, Somali, Galla, and Konso. In addition tables for Hadiyya and Dullay will be presented; although these languages are not among the best attested varieties of EC, it was felt that their respective sound histories are sufficiently well known to counterbalance the one-sided picture offered by the "Lowland-East-Cushitic" languages.

(1)  SAHO-AFAR

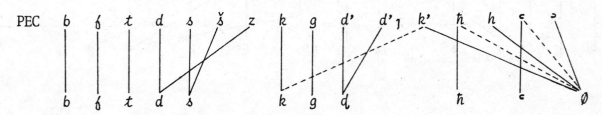

(2)  SOMALI

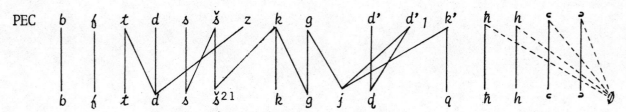

(3)  GALLA

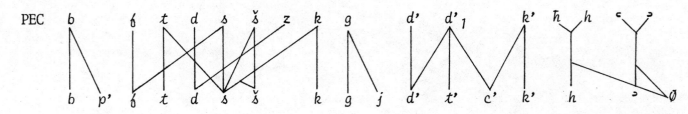

(4)  KONSO

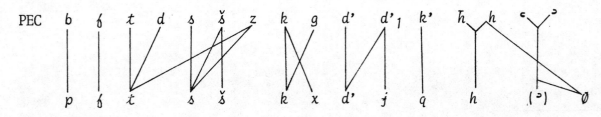

---

[21]Later on → *y*.

(5)  DULLAY (Gawwada and Gollango)[22]

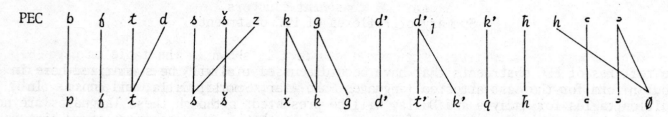

(6)  HADIYYA

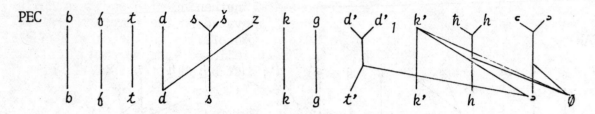

---

[22]The correspondences are essentially the same for all Dullay languages; Harso and Dobase differ from the above in the following minor points:  *k'* occurs instead of *q*, *c'* instead of *k'*; *\*t* becomes *c*, while *\*d* becomes *t*; *\*k* becomes *h*.

## APPENDIX C

### Summary of consonant clusters

The total amount of reconstructed consonant clusters is shown in the table on page 58. Most of these clusters and their individual reflexes have already been discussed in the relevant chapters; in the following we will examine some possible generalizations about the phonotactic structure of PEC.

The lack of the geminate cluster *tt* is certainly fortuitous; the lack of geminate laryngeals and pharyngeals may however constitute an indication that such clusters were not part of the morpheme structure of PEC. Morphophonemic lengthening of *ħ* and *ʕ* in Dullay, and of *h* and *ʔ* in Konso-Gidole may perhaps have been innovated on the general model of morphophonemic gemination ( as a means of plural formation etc.). On the other hand, if these morphophonemic geminations are taken to represent relics of the morphological pattern of PEC (and they certainly must be so interpreted), it must be admitted that PEC has at least deep structure geminates of all possible consonants.

The non-occurrence of clusters such as *td*, *dt*, *ts*, *st*, *ɟb*, *bɟ*, *sz* etc. can be subsumed under the following general statement: segments of the same articulation point which differ only in voice and/or fricativity will not cluster. There was, however, the cluster *s* + *t* with a morpheme boundary in between; it can be assumed that the assimilation of this cluster to *ss* was already underway in PEC (cf. 4.16), although it was repeatedly restituted for reasons of paradigm consistency.

Clusters containing *t* are extremely rare. Only very few examples of clusters with *t* as a first member have been found, such as *\*th* in *\*math-* 'head', and no cluster with *t* as its second member has been reconstructed. This is probably due to the weak resistance of *t* against assimilations; in this connection it is interesting to note that in at least three unrelated instances an earlier *t* has given rise to an archi-consonant that fully assimilates to all preceding or following consonants: the reflexive *t* in Saho-Afar, the second person suffix *-tV* in Dasenech, and the *t* of the second person selector *\*ʔat* in Konso-Gidole and in Dullay.

There are relatively few examples of stop clusters other than geminates. This may also be due to assimilatory tendencies in the proto-language, though no solid indications of such processes can be found. The cluster *\*tb* may be reconstructed for Somali *udub*, Galla *utub-a* 'roof-pole' (*\*ʔutb-*), though only on the assumption of echo-vowel epenthesis. The reconstruction of *\*dk* and *\*dg* is not solidly supported; all previous reconstructions with *\*dg* and *\*dk* such as *\*midg-* 'right' and *\*ħidk-* 'star' (cf. Black 1974) under these items) have turned out to represent *\*zg* and *\*zk*, respectively. Only *\*ʔudg-* 'fragrance' (Somali *udg-oon*, Galla *urg-aw-* 'exhale fragrance') may be a case in point, but unfortunately the reflexes are ambiguous as to *\*d* or *\*z*. The same is true of the cluster *\*db* in Galla *garb-uu* 'barley', Konso *kapp-a* and Gidole *kapp(-o)* 'wheat' (Black *\*gadb-* 1974:180), which turned out to represent *\*zb* on the evidence of Gawwada, Harso and Gollango *kasp-o* 'wheat'. There is one instance for which the reconstruction of a cluster *\*bdʼ* seems appropriate: Som. *libḍ-* 'vanish, disappear' = Konso *libbʼ-* 'id.', PEC *\*libdʼ-*. This is an interesting example of how earlier consonant clusters may contribute to the development of new phonemes (in this case Konso *bʼ*, which is not directly derivable from any PEC phoneme).

As can be seen from the table on page 58, clusters with sonorants as either first or second member are exceedingly frequent. These are generally retained as such, except that in Galla all obstruents become nasals before nasals. The clusters *mm*, *nn*, and *mn* are thus highly ambiguous in Galla:

| 2nd \ 1st | t | k | ʔ | b | d | g | d' | $d'_1$ | k' | ɓ | s | š | h | ħ | z | ʕ | m | n | l | r | w | y |
|---|---|---|---|---|---|---|---|---|---|---|---|---|---|---|---|---|---|---|---|---|---|---|
| t |  |  |  | + |  |  |  |  |  |  |  |  |  | + | + |  | + |  |  |  |  |  |
| k |  | + |  |  |  |  |  |  |  |  |  |  |  | + | + |  | + | + |  |  |  |  |
| ʔ |  | + |  | + |  |  |  |  | + |  |  |  |  |  | + | + |  |  |  |  |  |  |
| b |  |  |  | + |  | + |  |  |  |  |  |  |  | + | + |  | + | + |  |  |  |  |
| d |  |  |  |  | + | + |  |  |  |  |  |  |  | + | + |  | + |  | + |  |  |  |
| g |  |  |  |  |  | + |  |  |  |  |  |  |  | + | + |  |  |  | + |  |  |  |
| d' |  |  |  |  |  | + |  |  | + |  |  |  |  | + | + |  |  |  |  |  |  |  |
| $d'_1$ |  |  |  |  |  |  |  |  |  |  |  |  |  |  |  |  |  |  |  |  |  |  |
| k' |  |  |  |  |  |  |  |  | + |  |  |  |  |  | + |  | + |  |  | + |  |  |
| ɓ |  |  |  |  |  |  | + |  |  |  |  | + |  |  | + |  |  |  |  | + |  |  |
| s |  |  |  | + |  |  | + | + | + |  | + |  |  | + |  | + |  |  |  | + |  |  |
| š |  |  |  |  |  |  |  |  |  |  |  |  |  | + |  |  |  |  |  |  |  |  |
| h |  |  |  |  | + |  |  |  |  |  |  |  |  |  |  |  | + |  |  |  |  |  |
| ħ |  |  |  |  |  |  |  |  |  |  |  |  |  |  |  |  | + |  | + |  |  |  |
| z | + |  |  | + |  | + |  |  |  |  |  |  |  | + | + | + | + |  |  |  |  |  |
| ʕ |  |  |  | + | + |  |  |  |  |  |  |  |  |  |  | + |  |  |  |  |  |  |
| m |  | + |  | + |  | + |  |  | + |  |  |  |  | + | + |  | + | + |  |  |  |  |
| n | + |  |  | + | + | + |  |  |  |  |  |  |  | + | + |  | + | + | + |  |  |  |
| l | + |  |  | + | + | + | + |  | + | + |  |  |  | + | + | + |  | + |  | + |  |  |
| r | + |  | + | + | + | + | + | + | + | + |  |  |  | + | + | + | + |  | + |  |  |  |
| w |  |  |  | + |  |  |  |  | + | + |  |  |  |  |  |  |  | + | + | + | + |  |
| y |  |  |  |  |  |  | + |  |  | + |  |  |  |  |  |  |  |  | + |  |  | + |

mm < *mm, *km, *k'm, *gm, *nm

nn < *tn, *dn, *d'n, *kn, *k'n, *gn, *nn, *zn

mn < *bn, *ɓn, *sn, *ṁn

For examples cf. the discussion of the items *ɭuk'm-, *zagm-, *wazn-, *ħubn-, *gabn- as well as the following cognate sets:

*gatn- 'rainy season': Gidole kašan 'large rainy season about Feb. past June', Gawwada katan-ko 'id.', Tsamay gatan-ko 'id.': Galla gann-a.

*ʔarag-naa 'we see': Somali arag-naa, Galla aran-na.

Contrary to the reflex of d/z and d' before n these consonants are not nasalized before m but display the usual r reflex otherwise found before obstruents (e.g. mirg-a 'right-hand' < *mizg-): *gudm- 'shoulder' → gurm-uu (Burji qudum-a, Hadiyya qudum-o), and hirm-aa 'bel[

< *ḥidʼ-m- from *ḥidʼ- 'tie'.

On the loss of laryngeals and eventually also pharyngeals in postconsonantal position cf. 4.17, 4.18, and 4.21).

In concluding, it must be said that the reconstruction of PEC consonant clusters is still in its inception and still deserves a lot of painstaking work.  The following are some hints for directions in future research.  First of all, it has proved possible that PEC possessed many more prefix verbs than any one of the individual languages including Saho and Afar.  Prefix verbs were of two types, biradical (with two root consonants), and triradical (with three root consonants).  One of the main characteristics of triradical verbs is their unusual root pattern CCVC.  Nominal derivations of such verbs (verbal nouns and adjectives), which normally continue as suffix verbs, are, however, of the pattern CVCC. A good example of this process is *-kʼsol- 'laugh' with its nominal derivation *kʼosl- 'laughing' (as a verbal adjective), 'laughter' (as a verbal noun).  The former is attested as a prefix verb in Saho (-oo-sol-) and Afar (-u-sul-) while the latter continues as a suffix verb in Somali, Galla, Konso etc.  A consequence of this bifurcating patterning is the fact that wherever prefix verbs underlie PEC roots, the same root consonants come to form different consonant clusters ($C_1C_2$ and $C_2C_3$), and the effects of changes in both clusters may continue into the individual languages.  Thus, Galla koɬl-, Konso xosal-, Gidole hols- etc. owe their k instead of *kʼ to an earlier rule which changed kʼ to k before ʂ in the variant *-kʼsol- (→ *-ksol-), although the variant which continues into these languages is undoubtedly the verbal adjective *kʼosl-.  It is possible in this way to reconstruct the exact shapes of certain roots on the basis of the different behavior of their constituent consonants in different clusters.  The following example may serve to illustrate this point.  Compare the root *nass-/*ness- reconstructed in 4.13, which was given the meaning 'breathe, rest'.  It is obvious, however, that the original PEC item underlying this cognate set was a noun, cf. Konso ness-a, Dullay nass-o 'soul, breath' etc. Even more specifically, it can be assumed that it was a nominal derivation of some prefix verb.  Saho, according to Reinisch, has a prefix verb -mʄes-/-mʄis- which would certainly fulfill the conditions required for a relationship with *nass-/*ness-, because it is morphophonemically /nfVs/ and possesses a verbal noun naʄs-e/neʄs-e.  Since no non-alternating roots with the cluster ʄs have been reconstructed, and since there is a certain amount of evidence from alternating roots that the cluster **ʄs became PEC *ss, it could conceivably be assumed that *nass-/*ness- derives from **naʄs-/**neʄs-, were it not for the fact that Saho nʄVs is usually treated as a loan from Semitic.  Borrowing is indeed a suggestive hypothesis, since both Ethiosemitic and Arabic possess this root.  On the other hand, we have Saho neʄ 'face' and Somali naʄ 'soul' which are not likely to have been borrowed from Semitic because of the lack of ʂ, and are obviously cognate with the items referred to above.  Regardless of whether or not Saho -nʄVs- is a loan from Semitic, the existence of these words clearly demonstrates the presence of an underlying ʄ in the proto-root.  While Saho neʄ and Somali naʄ may be assumed to derive from a metathesized variant *neʄs-, PEC *nass-/*ness- appears to continue the normal verbal noun *naʄs-/*neʄs-.

A second possible way of reconstructing consonant clusters in PEC is that of comparing bisyllabic bases with echo-vowel epenthesis with their monosyllabic alternants, as was done in the case of *gatn-.  In none of the daughter languages is the cluster *tn retained as such; it can indeed be assumed to have merged with *nn prior to the split of PEC into the individual languages.  It is nevertheless possible to reconstruct the cluster *tn by way of comparison plus morphophonemic considerations:  the alternant pair *gatan-/*gann- cannot have any underlying representation other than *gatn-.

# APPENDIX D

## Index of PEC reconstructions

*ˀaab-/*ˀabb- 'father' 15

*-a(a)w- denominative morpheme 44, 46

*ˀaayy- 'mother' 44

*ˀaƒ- 'mouth' 19, 51

*ˀamm(-an)- 'time, now' 25

*ˀarb- 'elephant' 14

*ˀarrab- (~ *ᶜarrab-) 'tongue' 23, 36, 54

*ˀat- 'thou' 10

*ˀatin-/*ˀitin- 'you' (pl.) 11

*ˀawr- 'large male animal' 45, 46

*-ayš- causative of denominative 44, 46

*-a-yt- singulative suff. 46

*ˀayy- (~ *ˀay-C) 'who, which' 46

*ˀayyaan- 'spirit, good luck' 44

*ˀerg- 'send' 17

*ˀil- 'eye' 5, 22

*ˀil/*ˀul- 'stick' 5

*ˀilk- 'tooth' 12, 22, 40

*ˀin(a)m- 'child' 24

*ˀis- 'self' 35, 54

*ˀiš-ii 'she' 34, 35

*-iš- causative suffix 35

*ˀool- 'stay' 51

*ˀooy- 'cry, weep' 43

*ˀorg- 'billy-goat' 23

*ˀudg- 'fragrance' 57

*ˀuƒƒ- 'blow' 19

*ˀus-ɯ 'he' 34

*ˀutb- 'roof-pole' 57


*ᶜag-/*ᶜig-/*ᶜug- 'drink' 17

*ᶜal- 'mountain, highland' 35, 36

*ᶜawl- 'yellow, brown' 46

*ᶜawš-/*ᶜayš- 'grass' 44, 45, 47

*ᶜazz- 'white' 36

*ᶜils-/*ᶜuls- 'heavy' 5, 6

*ᶜol- 'war' 21


*baabb- 'daddy' 44

*baˀ- 'become destroyed' 50, 52

*baˀk-/*buˀk- 'illness' 53

*bad- 'get lost' 14

*bahal- 'wild animal' 41

*bak'- 'crush' 48, 49

*bald-/*ballaad'- 'broad' 7, 22

*bark'-/*birk'- 'lightning' 49

*bar(-r)- 'time' 14

*baz- 'lake, sea' 20

*beel- 'lose' 54

*bidħ- 'left side' 16

*bik-ee 'water' 13

*bis- 'flower, color' 14, 32

*biy- 'earth' 45

*bohl- 'hole' 16, 41

*bok'l- 'hundred' 48


*daˀ- 'rain; overflow' 52, 53

*dab-/*dib-/*dub- 'back, tail' 15, 16

*dak'- 'come; go' 49

*darᶜ- 'ashes' 16

*dey-/*doy- 'look at' 16, 44

*diid- 'refuse' 16

*dikk'-/*dukk'- 'small' 50

*door- 'choose' 23

*dub- 'bake' 54

*d'agħ-   'stone'  18

*d'aħl-   'inherit'  36

*d'al-   'beget, give birth'  21, 30

*d'amħ-   'cold'  25, 26, 36, 54

*d'aw-   'hit, strike'  43

*d'awr-   'prevent'  46

*d'azk-   'female'  41

*d'eg-/*d'og-  'hear'  17

*-d'h-   'say'  41

*d'ib-   'cover; bury'  54

*d'ibb-   'hundred'  26, 29

*d'iit-   'kick'  26, 30

*d'ink-/*d'unk-  'kiss'  26

*d'iš-   'plant, build'  26, 30, 33

*d'ug-   'truth'  26

*d'uus-   'fart'  26

*d'₁aal-   'exceed'  27

*d'₁aɓ-   'meadow'  27

*d'₁ak'-/*d'₁ik'-  'wash'  29, 30

*d'₁eer-   'be ashamed'  27

*d'₁iɓr-   'braid'  27, 29

*d'₁iib-   'squeeze, press'  29, 30

*d'₁i(i)ɓ-  'grow tall, stretch oneself'  27, 29

*d'₁iir-   'male'  30

*d'₁ikl-   'elbow'  30

*d'₁ilħ-/*d'₁ulħ-  'charcoal'  22, 30

*d'₁ookk'-  'mud'  30, 50

*d'₁ub-   'dip in'  30

*d'₁uɓ-   'close, shut'  29, 31

*d'₁ur-   'be dirty'  29, 31

*ɓal-   'curse, bewitch, deceive'  18, 38

*ɓald'₁-  'log; split (wood)'  31

*ɓanħ-   'opening' → 'gap, space, interval'  38

*ɓiik'-   'sweep'  48, 49, 50

*ɓil-   'comb'  19

*ɓur-   'open, free, untie'  19

*ɓuud'₁-  'whistle'  29

*gaas-   'horn'  33, 44

*gabn-   'dainty'  15, 58

*gal-   'enter, go home'  17

*ganᶜ-   '(palm of) hand'  17, 36, 54

*gasar-   'buffalo'  33

*gat-   'sell'  10

*gatn-   'rainy season'  58, 59

*gawraᶜ-  'cut throat'  45

*gaws-   'molar'  45

*gay-   'arrive'  43

*gazb-   'barley or wheat'  57

*geᶜl-   'love'  18, 36

*gelz-   'baboon'  18, 20

*gerᶜ-   ? 'old'  37

*gidd-   'middle'  16, 18

*gilb-/*gulb-  'knee'  5, 6, 18

*gir-   'live, exist'  18

*god-   'hole (in the ground), cave'  16

*goy-   ? 'cut'  44

*guʾ-   'rainy season; year'  53

*gub-   'mountain'  15

*gub-   'burn'  17

*gudd-/*guud-  'big'  16

*gudm-   'shoulder'  58

*guyy-   'day'  44

*ha   jussive particle  39

*habaar-   'curse'  39, 40

*haɓɓ-   'drown'  39

*hagoog-   'drape cloth over head'  39, 40

*hal-   'she-camel'  37, 39, 40

*hamhaam-   'yawn'  39, 40

*har-   'become tired or weak'  40

*har- 'pond, creek' 39, 40

*haš- 'hold, keep' 39

*hawn-/*haween- 'night' 40

*-hdir-/*-hdur- 'sleep' 41 (cf. *hudr-)

*hebel- 'what's-his-name' 38, 40

*heg-/*hog- 'be erect, stand' 39

*hinaas- 'be jealous' 40

*hor- 'be in front' 40

*hub- 'injure' ? 40

*hub- 'know, be sure' 38, 40, 41

*hudr- 'sleep' 40 (cf. *-hdir-/*-hdur-)

*hur- 'recover from illness' 39, 40

*hurguƨ- 'shake off' 38

*huww- 'dress, wear' 38

*ħadd'- 'bitter' 54

*ħam-/*ħum- 'bad' 38

*ħand'ur-/*ħund'ur- 'navel' 24, 30, 39

*ħarr- 'donkey' 39

*ħawl-/*ħawaal-/*ħawwaal- 'grave, bury' 6, 43, 44

*ħayd'- 'fat' 46

*ħek'-/*ħok'- 'scratch' 48, 50

*ħid'- 'tie' 36, 59

*ħizk-/*ħuzk- 'star' 11, 35, 36, 37, 39, 57

*ħizz- 'root' 20, 36

*ħubn- 'muscle' ? 15, 58

*kaᶜ- 'get up' 11, 12, 36, 54

*kal- 'kidney' 12

*kal- 'yesterday' 9

*kan(n)-/*kinn- 'bee' 6, 24

*kaww- 'alone' 44

*kebᶜ- 'leopard' 13, 54

*ken- 'five' 12, 13

*kebeel- ( < *kebᶜ-eel-) 'leopard' 12, 13, 37

*ker- 'dog' 13

*kesƨ- 'chest' 54

*ki/*ku 'thee' 13

*kilm- 'tick' 13

*kils- 'fat' (adj.) 41 (cf. *-klis-/*-klus-)

*kimbir- 'small bird' 13, 15

*kir-/*kor-/*kur- 'circular formation' 5, 9

*kirb- 'dance and sing' 12, 13

*-klis-/*-klus- 'be fat' 41 (cf. *kils-)

*kob- 'sandal' 12

*kool- 'feather, wing' 11

*ku, acc. *ka, masc. demonstr.

*kub- 'pour' 8, 13

*kuƨ- 'fall' 11, 54

*kum- 'thousand' 12, 25

*kurd'$_1$uum-/*murkuud'$_1$- 'fish' 29, 31

*kut- 'dog' 12

*kuy- 'anthill' 43, 45

*k'a(a)w- 'hole' 43

*k'ab- 'catch, have' 14, 48

*k'ab- 'cold' 49

*k'adħ-/*k'udħ- 'thorn' 49

*k'ad'$_1$- 'cut' 31, 48

*k'ah- 'flee' 41

*k'al- 'slaughter' 49

*k'all- (*k'aℓ'- ?) 'thin, insignificant' 22, 48

*k'aniin- 'bite' 25

*k'ar- 'point, peak, top' 48

*k'ar- 'sharp' 49

*k'awᶜ- 'thunder' 47, 48

*k'eb- 'break' 49

*k'er-/*k'uur- 'cut' 5

*k'olɓ-    'bark (of tree)'  22, 48

*k'om-    'chew, bite, eat'  25

*-k'(o)m-        'id.'  25

*k'or-    'wood, tree'  48, 49

*k'osl-    'laugh(ing)'  41, 48, 49, 59

*k'ot-    'dig'  10

*k'oyy-    'wet'  49

*-k'sol-    'laugh'  25, 41, 48, 59

*k'ub-    'finger'  49, 54

*k'uɓ(a)ᶜ-    'cough'  19, 36, 48, 54

*laᵊb-/*labᵊ-    'breast-bone'  53

*laɓ-    'bone'  21

*lak-/*lik-/*luk-    'foot, leg'  5, 12, 41

*lakk-    'both, twin'  12, 20

*lam(m)-    'two'  21, 25

*lawx-    ? 'arrow'  21

*leᵊ-    'die' (pl. subject)  22, 52

*leᶜ-    'moon'  21, 36

*leb-    'big, male'  22

*leh-    'having'  41

*libd'-    'disappear'  57

*liħ-    'six'  22, 36

*lik'-/*luk'-    'swallow'  49

*loᵊ-    'cows'  52, 53

*lukk-    'chicken'  12

*luk'm-    'neck'  21, 49, 58

*ma(ᵊ)  negative particle  52

*magᶜ-    'name'  17, 36

*magin-    'foot'  54

*malab-    'honey'  14

*malħ-    'pus'  5, 21, 35, 36

*man-/*min-  'house'  24

*mar-    'round'  24

*matħ-    'head'  5, 8, 10, 36, 37, 54, 57

*-mg-    'fill'  25

*mid'₁-    'fruit'  29

*mig-/*mug-  'fullness'  25

*mik'-    'bone'  49

*mizg-    'right side'  25, 57, 58

*mudᶜ-    'stab'  37

*mur-    'cut'  23

*murkuud'₁-  cf. *kurd'₁uum-

*murk'-    'gristle'  54

*naᵊs-    'woman's breast'  52

*nab-    'smear'  24

*nabħ-    'ear'  24

*nagay-    'peace, health'  43

*naħ-    'fear'  23

*nam-/*nim-/*num-  'man'  24

*nass-/*ness-  'breathe, rest'  23
        (< *naɓs-/*neɓs-  59)

*naxɓ-    ? 'body'  21

*-nᶜeb-    'hate'  23

*neᶜb-    'hated'  14, 23

*nuug-    'suck'  24

*raɓ-    'sleep'  22

*rah-    'frog'  41

*-rd-    'run'  23

*riᵊ-    'goat'  22, 53

*riɓ-    'pluck'  19

*riɓ-an-    'hair'  19

*roob-    'rain'  22

*saal-    'cow-dung'  32

*saᵊ-    'morning'  52

*saᵊn-    'footprint, heel'  52

*san-/*sin-/*son-/*sun-  'nose'  5, 24

*sar-/*ser-/*sir-/*sur-  'relative'  5

*seg-/*sog-  'far'  5, 54

*sibᵊ-/*subᵊ-  'slippery; mud'  53

*sind'₁- 'urine' 24

*sirn-/*surn- 'nasal mucus' 23, 32

*sọˀ- 'meat' 50, 52

*sooh- 'twist' 12, 41

*sun(u)n- 'nose-bleeding' 32


*šaᶜ- 'cow' 36

*šaal- 'oryx' 33

*šeeb- 'leather strap' 33

*šok'- 'beat, hit' 33

*šor- 'rich' 33

*šuᶜs- 'smell' 33


*-tak'-/*-tuk'- 'touch, push,
     strike' 48

*tir- 'liver' 11

*tom(m)an-/*tomn- 'ten' 10, 25

*tuf- 'spit' 10

*tum- 'pound, beat, forge' 10, 24


*waak'- 'sky-god' 42, 49

*waal- 'hand-clapping game' 42

*waay- 'fail' 42

*waᶜ- 'shout, call, invite' 42

*war- 'news' 42

*war- 'river' 42

*waraab- 'hyena' 42

*waraab- 'draw water' 42

*warħan- 'spear' 37

*warš- 'rhinoceros' 33, 54

*wayn- 'big' 42

*wazn- 'heart' 20, 58

*weger- ? 'olive tree' 42

*wisl- 'dream' 43


*yaad- 'think, worry' 43

*yaal-/*yeel- 'do' (involuntarily) 43

*yaayy- 'mama' 44, 45

*yerg- 'axe' 43

*yeyy-/*yoyy- 'wild dog' 43

*yug- 'pull off, out' 43


*zagm- 'honey' 20, 54, 58

*zak- 'swim' 12

*zit- 'pull' 20

*-zrig-/*-zrug- 'move, push' ? 20

# REFERENCES

Abraham, R.C.   1962.   *Somali-English Dictionary*.   London.

Amborn, H., G. Minker and H.J. Sasse.   Forthcoming.   *Das Dullay. Materialien zu einer ostkuschitischen Sprachengruppe*.   Kölner Beiträge zur Afrikanistik, vol. 6.

Andrzejewski, B.W.   1957.   "Some preliminary observations on the Borana Dialect of Galla."   *BSOAS* 19:354-74.

Andrzejewski, B.W.   1960.   "The categories of number in noun forms in the Borana Dialect of Galla."   *Africa* 30:62-75.

Andrzejewski, B.W.   1962.   "Ideas about warfare in Borana Galla stories and fables."   *AfrLS* 3:116-36.

Andrzejewski, B.W.   1970.   "The role of tone in the Borana Dialect of Galla."   *Proceedings of the Third International Conference of Ethiopian Studies, Addis Ababa 1966*, vol 2.   Addis Ababa.   88-98.

Anttila, R.   1972.   *An Introduction to Historical and Comparative Linguistics*.   New York.

Armstrong, L.   1934.   *The Phonetic Structure of Somali*.   Mitteilungen des Seminars für Orientalische Sprachen zu Berlin, Jahrgang 37, Abteilung 3, 116-61.

Bell, C.R.V.   1953.   *The Somali Language*.   London.

Bender, M.L.   1971.   "The languages of Ethiopia:   A new lexicostatistical classification and some problems of diffusion."   *AL* 13:165-388.

Bender, M.L., ed.   1976.   *The Non-Semitic Languages of Ethiopia*.   Monograph No. 5, Occasional Papers Series, Committee on Ethiopian Studies, African Studies Center, Michigan State University, East Lansing.

Black, P.   1972.   "Cushitic and Omotic classification."   *Language Sciences* 23:27-8.

Black, P.   1973a.   Ms.   "Draft sketch of Konso phonology, morphology, and syntax."

Black, P.   1973b.   Ms.   "Preliminary draft of a Gidole dictionary."

Black, P.   1974.   Doctoral dissertation.   "Lowland East Cushitic:   reconstruction and subgrouping."   University of Yale.

Black, P.   1975.   "Linguistic evidence on the origins of the Konsoid peoples."   *Proceedings of the First U.S. Conference on Ethiopian Studies, 1973*, ed. by H.G. Marcus.   Monograph No. 3, Occasional Papers Series, Committee on Ethiopian Studies, African Studies Center, Michigan State University, East Lansing.   291-302.

Black, P.   1976.   "Werizoid."   Chapter 10 in Bender, ed., 222-31.

Black, P. and Shako Otto.   1973.   Ms.   "Preliminary draft of a Konso dictionary."

Bliese, L.   1967.   Master's thesis.   "Selected problems in noun morphology in the Aussa Dialect of Afar."   University of Texas.

Bynon, J. and T. Bynon, eds.   *Hamito-Semitica. Proceedings of a Colloquium held by the Historical Section of the Linguistics Association (Great Britain) and the School of Oriental and African Studies, University of London, on the 18th, 19th, and 20th of March 1970*.   The Hague.   1975.

Cerulli, E.   1938.   *La Lingua e la storia dei Sidamo*.   Roma.

Da Thiene, G.   1939.   *Dizionario della lingua Galla*.   Harar.

Dolgopolskiy, A.B.   1973.   *Sravnitelno-istoričeskaya fonetika kušitskikh yazíkov*.   Moskva.

Fleming, H.C.   1964.   "Baiso and Rendille: Somali outliers."   *Rassegna di Studi Etiopici* 20:35-96.

Hayward, R.   1974.   "The segmental phonemes of Afar."   BSOAS 38:385-406.

Heine, B.   1973.   "Vokabulare ostafrikanischer Restsprachen I: Elmolo."   *Afrika und Übersee* 56:276-83.

Heine, B.   1974.   "Notes on the Yaaku Language (Kenya)."   *Afrika und Übersee* 58:27-61, 119

Heine, B.   1975.   "Notes on the Rendille Language (Kenya)."   *Afrika und Übersee* 59:176-223.

Heine, B.   1977.   "Bermerkungen zur Elmolo-Sprache."   *Afrika und Übersee* 59:278-99.

Heine, B.   1978a.   "Bermerkungen zur Boni-Sprache."   *Afrika und Übersee* 60:242-95.

Heine, B.   1978b.   "The Sam languages. A history of Rendille, Boni and Somali."   *Afroasiatic Linguistics* 6/2:23-115.

Linton, G., R. Kaley and D. Collidge.   Undated.   Unpublished word lists of South Ethiopian languages.

Luc, (Père).   1967.   *Vocabulaire ᶜafar*.   Djibouti.

Mahaffy, F.E.   Undated.   "An outline of the phonemics and morphology of the Afar (Dankali) languages of Eritrea, East Africa."   Addis Ababa (mimeo.).

Moreno, M.M.   1939.   *Grammatica teorico-pratica della lingua galla*.   Milano.

Moreno, M.M.   1940.   *Manuale di Sidamo*.   Milano.

Moreno, M.M.   1951.   "Brevi notazioni di Ǧiddu."   *Rassegna di Studi Etiopici* 10:99-107.

Palmer, F.R.   1970.   "Cushitic."   In T.A. Seboek, ed., *Current Trends in Linguistics, Vol. 6: Linguistics in South West Asia and North Africa*.   The Hague.   571-85.

Plazikowski-Brauner, H.   1960.   "Die Hadiya-Sprache."   *Rassegna di Studi Etiopici* 16:83-115.

Plazikowski-Brauner, H.   1964.   "Wörterbuch der Hadiya-Sprache."   *Rassegna di Studi Etiopici* 20:133-82.

Reinisch, L.   1885-7.   *Die ᶜAfar-Sprache*.   Wien.

Reinisch, L.   1890.   *Die Saho-Sprache, vol. 2: Wörterbuch*.   Wien.

Sasse, H.-J.   1973.   "Spuren von Pharyngalen im Galab."   *Afrika und Übersee* 56:266-75.

Sasse, H.-J.   1974a.   "Notes on the Structure of Galab."   BSOAS 37:407-38.

Sasse, H.-J.   1974b.   "Kuschitistik 1972."   In W. Voigt, ed., XVIII. *Deutscher Orientalistentag 1972 in Lübeck - Vorträge*.   Wiesbaden.   618-28.

Sasse, H.-J.   1975.   "Galla /š/, /s/ und /f/."   *Afrika und Übersee* 58:244-63.

Sasse, H.-J.   1976a.   "Weiteres zu den ostkuschitischen Sibilanten."   *Afrika und Übersee* 59:125-42.

Sasse, H.-J.   1976b.   "Dasenech."   Chapter 9 in Bender, ed., 196-221.

Sasse, H.-J.   Forthcoming.   "The extension of Macro-Somali."   *Colloque international sur les langues couchitiques*, Paris 1975 (to appear in the Proceedings).

Sasse. H.-J., and H. Straube.   1977.          "Kultur und Sprache der Burji in Süd-Äthiopien: Ein Abriss."   In Möhlig, W.J.G. et al, eds., *Zur Sprachgeschichte und Ethnohistoirie in Afrika*.   Berlin: Reimer.   Pp. 239-66.

Welmers, Wm. E.   1952.   "Notes on the structure of Saho."   *Word* 8:145-62, 236-81.

Zaborski, A.  1970.  "Cushitic languages—an unexplored subcontinent."  *Bulletin of the International Committee on Urgent Anthropological and Ethnological Research* 12:118-28.

Zaborski, A.  1976.  "Cushitic overview."  Chapter 4 in Bender, ed., 67-84.